HOW
MENTAL HEALTH
SAVAGE

By

Tami **O**dimayo

Dedication

To my loving father,

Ayo Odimayo

Thank you for letting me switch my major to Psychology lol

Visit our Website www.TamiTalks.com

First Edition: October 2020

ISBN: 9798692342911
Imprint: Independently published

Printed in the United States of America

Other Books by Tami Odimayo

- Olivetti: Inception
- Olivetti: Illumination
- Olivetti: Inferno
- Game of Confessions
- Diary of a Psychopath
- Relationship Code

Hello everyone,

My name is Tamilore Odimayo, your favorite therapist. In my short life, I have grown to enjoy writing and counseling. I am thrilled to be able to combine both in the form of a book. My intent is that this book becomes a living way people get help from one another. For instance, if you struggle with depression, you can find out how others have coped or are coping.

*You are not required to read the book page by page to find results. Preferably you should read the table of contents, find out what you need for **today**, follow the suggestions and partake in the challenges. You may only need two tips, or you may need all. Let us create a community of Mental Health warriors, advocates, and SAVAGES.*

Thank you,

Tamilore Odimayo, LCPC, CADC

#MentalHealthTipsfromTami

One of the key ways to help your mental health is to interact with others. It is in our genetic nature to socialize because isolation is not in our nature. Our entire life is based on human connection.

To foster this principle, I created intractable Hashtags to apply to your social media account. These hashtags can be used on Instagram, Twitter, and Facebook. If you don't have any social media account, you can google the hashtags to find tips others have benefited from.

For instance, one of the primary hashtags that will be used in all chapters is #MentalHealthTipsfromTami. You can google this or search this on your social media platform, and you will find some helpful videos, providing these tips.

Have fun with the book and learn how others cope with day to day mental health stressors by using and searching the hashtags in each chapter.

Contents

Prologue

#MentalHealthTipsfromTami

Mental health as a science is a recent phenomenon. In the early centuries, most mental illnesses were seen as demonic possessions. People with symptoms similar to Schizophrenia, Bipolar Disorder, and Depression were treated with Christian or other religious rituals. In fact, if you accidentally talked to something or someone that was not physically present, you would most likely be considered a witch. And we know history has not been kind to witches.

As time went by, mental health graduated towards becoming a science and researchable discipline—things began to change.

Doctors and Therapists transited from inhumane treatment of mental health disorders and moved towards a more therapeutic way. Asylums are no longer the way they used to be. Medical and therapeutic interventions have been growing exponentially. Now, a person with schizophrenia, who doesn't pose harm to themselves or society, can live a normal life with the right medications and therapeutic procedures. Other diagnoses like Major Depression, Generalized Anxiety Disorder, Panic Disorder, Bipolar Disorder, etc. can all be treated with effective interventions.

Despite this, the field of Mental Health still has a stigma attached to it. I have met many people who do not want others knowing they see a Therapist or Psychiatrist. I have also met individuals who don't prioritize their mental health as effectively as their physical health. A majority of individuals with health insurance never miss a yearly physical checkup, but never think about having an annual mental health check-up. It is sad to watch because research is now beginning to show that mental, physical, and spiritual health are intertwined. The mind-soul-body phenomenon is real.

Luckily, the Mental Health field is beginning to erupt with soldiers we call Advocates. Our goal is to bring Mental Health awareness to light. Our goal is to help others understand that it is okay not to be okay. It is okay to ask for help. There is no shame in identifying a persistent problem you're facing. There is no shame in working with a professional to ease the emotional discomfort you are feeling. Unlike physical health, mental health is a silent killer. It has caused multiple suicides and homicides. It has destroyed many families and many relationships. Most importantly, unmanaged mental health has the capability of destroying an individual's sense of self.

If you're struggling with addiction or any mental health symptom, remember that you are not alone. You are not weird. No one will laugh or mock you, and the ones that do, do so because they are just not AWARE. At the end of the day, you know you more than anyone knows you. You know when something is not right with your well-being. However, you may not know that you can achieve a level of happiness regardless of your circumstances. It is not a comfortable journey, but it is worth taking the first step.

#MentalHealthAwareness #MentalHealthSavage

The basic principle of mental health

This book's principles are guaranteed to change your thought process about your mental health and provide you with concrete ways to help yourself through many mental health stressors.

When you apply it, the sky is the limit!

I'm not going to lie. My mental health journey has been filled with roadblocks. Through clinical knowledge and experiential knowledge, I came up with these principles, and they have helped me tremendously. However, it is crucial to understand that mental health, like any other health condition, requires a combination of lifestyle changes, possibly medications, and definitely seeking a Therapist #MyMentalHealthJourney

Descartes had a famous quote that a lot of people have not fully grasped. He said, "I think; therefore, I am." This simple quote is the basis of human existence. Everything we act on, feel and experience, starts with a thought.

Our thought is what makes us, us. Our thought is what drives our desires, accomplishments, needs, wants, and being. Our thoughts make us different from others. Everyone's thoughts have a unique pattern.

Okay, why does this matter? Well, I'll tell you. Life happens because of our patterns of thinking. Our patterns of thinking determine what our mental health will be. That is why one of the most famous styles of therapy is Cognitive

Behavioral Therapy. Clinicians realize that if you can change a client's thought process, the behaviors will change, and life outcomes will definitely change.

One of the Universal Laws is the Law of Attraction. The Law of Attraction simply states that our dominant thought controls our lives and reality.

In my early career as a Therapist, I have come across several people I call "Positivity Vampires." These are people who hate summer, winter, spring, fall, ice cream, Krispy Kreme Donuts—everything! These individuals can never be satisfied. These individuals suck the life out of everything. You know who I am talking about. Yes! That one aunt that kills the vibe anytime she walks into a family event. That one neighbor that wants to call the cops anytime you have more than two cars parked in the driveway. Positivity vampires are everywhere.

Whenever I realize I am dealing with a Positive Vampire, the first thing I do is focus on what is going well in the moment.

If you are reading this, you might think it is simple to focus on the good. But for someone struggling with Major Depression, identifying why a Red Rose is beautiful is tough. My goal is not to focus on past problems during the first few sessions. My goal is to start to help the client see "the good" in the moment. For instance, I would ask, "What do you like about your shoes?"

Or "what are you grateful for today?"

When I ask these questions, I can literally observe a physical change. It first starts with a look of confusion. Like, "Why is this African Therapist asking me dumb questions?" then it turns to "Hmm, I never really thought that I could be grateful to have shoes to wear."

A mental shift is observed. The human body hates

negativity, and constant negativity will not only affect your mental health, but it will also definitely affect your physical health.

So, in summary, there is no basic principle(s) of mental health. There is one principle of mental health, and that is, *Be Aware of your Thoughts.* Be aware of what you allow into your mind. Religious texts talk about this principle. Your thoughts have to be managed. This may not be easy, but it is achievable by applying all the rules below.

Chapter 1

IT IS OKAY TO ASK FOR HELP

#AskforHelp

Asking for help isn't a sign of weakness

#AskforHelp

If you are moving a grand piano into your new apartment, you have two choices. You can do it yourself and risk potential harm to your back and the piano, or you can ask for help from one or more individuals.

Maintaining consistent mental health requires the ability to ask for help when needed willingly. In twelve-step programs, asking for help is highly valued. Asking for help is not just about humility; it is about forming a connection. Unfortunately, in today's individualistic society, asking for help has become a sign of weakness. Individuals are suffering psychologically, socially, and physically because of this.

Most individuals in their early twenties are quick to want to live by themselves. The promotion of the idea that you have to leave your parents' house at a certain age has caused many young twenty-somethings more difficulties in dealing with life.

What's wrong with staying at your parents for a while to build your savings account?

What's wrong with being roommates with a sibling or a

friend, to manage expenses?

I have met individuals who would rather have two jobs to pay for an apartment that they barely sleep in than have an extra roommate.

In life, asking for help comes in different forms, but the most necessary form is when it comes to your mental health.

- How many times have you called a friend to just talk about your feelings?
- How many times have you asked your friend if you can help them with their emotions?
- At what point is it okay to admit that everything going on in your life right now is unmanageable?
- At what point is it okay to admit that maybe I need help from a Therapist or other mental health professional?

Problems with asking for help mostly occur in the male population. Research shows that the male population is experiencing a weird disconnect caused by years of improper socialization. Men see asking for help as a weakness. Men see the expression of certain emotions as weakness.

How many times have you heard, "men don't cry."? Men are supposed to man up, deal with it, suck it up, and fix it. Years of this dialogue have made men at a higher risk of attempting and committing suicide.

If you are reading this, know that it is okay not to be okay. Know that your worth is not based on how well you can deal with problems yourself, but how well you can utilize your natural need to connect with others to achieve balance.

Let someone help you with that piano called trauma, stress, depression, grief, etc. Every great leader knows that humans are stronger together than apart.

Quick tips:

Tami Odimayo

1. Apply the tips in this book.
2. You should always have at least five reliable people on your support system.
3. Each therapist has a unique style of therapy. Find a therapist that matches your personality and culture.
4. If you can't do it by yourself, before you second guess yourself, ask for help.
5. Be okay with people telling you "No" when you ask for help. It is part of life. Keep trying, and someone will eventually say, "Yes."
6. Be the friend that you want. If you want someone checking in on you to find out how you are doing, check in on them also.

Mental Health Savage Challenge

Call a friend or family member that you haven't spoken to in a while. Make a post about how asking for help has benefited you in the past month #AskforHelp

Find a therapeutic healer

The type of healer you seek depends on your personality, your culture, your access to services, your financial means, and what makes you comfortable. Besides clinical mental health therapists or counselors, there are other types of emotional healers.

For example, in 2018, I struggled with the most debilitating form of anxiety I had ever felt. It was even more debilitating because no one around me noticed. My body was silently destroying itself from the inside, and all I could think about every day was finding mental silence.

I thought I could "heal" myself. After all, I was a Therapist and helped others. I tried applying the coping skills I taught others in counseling sessions, and my anxiety somewhat reduced but was still there. I tried medications. I tried it for one day and hated the way I felt. I was so unusually calm. It made me question everything and eventually did the opposite.

I realized that the only thing I hadn't done was to see a Therapist. My pride told me that there was nothing a Therapist could say to me that I didn't already know. Then I asked around and found out that 80% of my Therapist colleagues had a Therapist also. I called my Doctor and told him to provide me with a referral. In minutes, I was given several options. I chose one, and till this day, I realized that *it was one of the best decisions I have ever made.*

Mental health is holistic. I had tried the diet, the spirituality, the neurobiological route, and still, nothing had worked. Once I added a Therapist, things changed. The more I dug deeper into the source of my anxiety, the easier my life became.

I then ventured to find other types of healers. For instance, I found a herb specialist who taught me how to utilize different teas to benefit my mental health. I am currently learning how to use earth stones etc.

My point is, different types of emotional healers can work well with different kinds of emotional needs.

A common statement I hear from those who avoid seeking emotional healers is,

"I have friends and family I can talk to, I don't need to see a specialist,"

That used to be me. Friends and family are an essential part of your support system. However, talking to a Therapist is different. An average Therapist/healer has had more than one hundred clients who have experienced various stressors. Over the course of practice, the healer has accumulated enough knowledge to understand what works and what doesn't work.

For instance, I have had several clients with relationship co-dependency. Because of this, I know what works and what doesn't work when it comes to practical communication setting and boundary setting.

Find a healer based on your preference and needs. Some of the options I have found helpful for my clients are hypnotists, energy healers, color therapy, acupuncture, craniosacral therapy, art therapy, faith therapy, pastors, light therapy, healing stones, etc. Find what you like and go with it.

Mental Health Savage Challenge

What type of healer have you found? How was it beneficial to you? What do you like about your healer? Make a video using #Findyourhealer.

Chapter 2
YOUR PHYSICAL HEALTH
#LivewithIntention

You are what you eat

Good mood, good food. This is one of my favorite chapters. Food brings humans together. It is the bond that we all have in common. It is our survival mechanism. It is how we experience connection. When we go on dates, the first thing that usually comes to mind is getting something to eat. When we have birthday celebrations, we think about food. When we have extended business meetings, we think about food. When it is nice and sunny outside, we think about barbequing some food. When it is cold, we think about making soup. Oh yes, and during major holidays like Thanksgiving and Christmas, it is all about food.

My point is food is everything. It is our source of energy, joy, connection, pleasure, and survival. If that is the case, we need to pay attention to what we eat, when we eat, and how we eat.

I went to a nutrition seminar that blew my mind. The whole seminar was about the significance of food for mental health. According to Pfeiffer's Law, "For every drug that benefits a patient, there is a natural substance that can achieve the same effect." Doctor Linus Pauling also proposed that mental abnormalities might be successfully treated by correcting nutritional imbalances in the body.

Thomas Edison's famously said, "The Doctor of the future will no longer treat the human frame with drugs but rather will cure and prevent disease with nutrition."

I am a firm believer that nature has given us every nutritional source that we need to survive, and that is why I tell everyone I know, "You are what you eat."

#youarewhatyoueat

A research done in a Spanish University showed that a Mediterranean Diet of fruits and vegetables, nuts and seeds, grains, fish, poultry, meat, olive oil, canola oil, and moderate use of wine caused a 50% reduction in Depression. Research has also shown that Vitamin D causes a significant decrease in seasonal depression.

Okay, enough with the research. Let us talk for real. What do you eat in the morning? What do you drink? What do you eat for lunch? How much water do you drink daily? What do you eat for dinner?

If your answer to any of this is junk food, soda, no water, excessive sugars, no vegetables or fruits, I am judging you a lot, jk.

Let us start this conversation with junk food like chips, cookies, popcorn, etc. Growing up, in college, and even at work, I see many people who skip a meal and take junk food from the vending machine instead. That is fine. There's nothing wrong with Junk food as long as it is not consistently replacing real food.

Why? Because those chemicals in the ingredient section, at the back of most junk food packages, are meant to preserve the shelf life of junk food, not yours. Those chemicals react with our natural body chemicals. It affects our moods and hormones. Our bodies are created to eat natural foods that are not processed excessively to have a three-year expiry date.

Food is meant to be fresh and then spoil. Fruits and foods are living beings. They produce the most nutrients when they are fresh and are repelling when their nutrients begin to deplete.

Simply put, it is okay to eat junk food as long as it is not done excessively, and it is not replacing a healthy meal.

Did you know that one 12 ounce can of soda contains 39 grams of sugar? And that is just what the label states (I am sure it is being downplayed). On a given outdoor event or even at a local restaurant, I observe people reach out for multiple rounds of soda. On average, if an individual goes for a refill, five times, that is 195g of sugar. #ProtestTheFoods

Many years ago, after watching a YouTube video of soda turning into black tar syrup, I decided I would quit taking soda due to the high sugar content. It was tough because part of my everyday routine involved soda. If I went to the gas station to refill my gas, I would buy a large soda for $1.50. If I went to a restaurant to eat, I would order some type of soda and have it refilled at least twice.

Quitting soda felt like a literal withdrawal from a drug, and that is because it is. I felt lethargic the first few weeks because my body was used to the sugar and caffeine bump. After two weeks, I began to drink more water. I realized I was less thirsty compared to when I drank soda. My memory was better. My digestive functioning was better. My sleep was better. My mood was better—everything was better. I felt clean and lighter on the inside. I lost significant excess weight and found it much easier to work out.

Water is life. A majority of your body is composed of water. Most foods naturally have water in them. Doctors recommend drinking sufficient water daily for health reasons. If you struggle with any mental health diagnosis, try reducing artificial sweeteners, sodas, and drinks.

Drink water instead. The results will be remarkable.

Nutritional scientists usually recommend eating fruits and vegetables in season. Remember when I said nature gives us everything we need? It really does.

A lot of clients I meet talk about their struggles with finding healthy foods to eat. Most grocery stores offer affordable non-organic options. The key is moderation. There are food pantries and places in your local communities that may provide food resources for you.

Jungle Diet

I want to use this opportunity to introduce the Jungle Diet to you. Like many of you reading this, I struggled with finding the ultimate diet. I have tried almost every diet known, and I find it troubling that most people don't realize that diet plans are not a one-size-fits-all plan. While some people may thrive in a diet like the Keto, others may not. In my quest to find out what works for me, I realized that individuals who eat natural foods tend to thrive more. So, I created rules for the jungle diet. #JungleDiet

#1. If you cannot cook it in the jungle, don't eat it. Aha! Yes! This number one rule eliminates chips, candy bars, soda, and all vending machine foods. It simply means, try your best to eat fresh. Try your best to eat something that can easily be cooked.

#2. Cook your food daily. The act of cooking is an energy transfer. If you cook while listening to music, you tend to enjoy the food better. Personally, I have noticed that when I eat fast food, I get anxious. The only reasonable explanation I have is that fast food is made in an anxious environment, and I'm ingesting that anxiety.

Also, in the jungle, there are no freezers. Because of this, you're forced to cook in exact portions, so there's no waste. Cooking daily allows you to portion your food. Some individuals use meal preps for food portioning to save time. The significant point here is to cook and portion your food, so you don't have to visit the fridge at one in the morning.

#3. Drink water. You can't find soda in the jungle. If you want something sweet, try iced tea, lemonade, or make natural smoothies. Make sure it is as natural as possible. P.S. there's tea for sleep, energy, constipation, anxiety, stress… everything. Honey sweetened tea is a better alternative to soda.

#4. If you live in the jungle, making food past a specific time of the day is not a good idea because it can attract wild animals. Generally, it is advisable to eat before sunset or a little bit after sunset. It gives your body time to digest your food before you go to bed.

#5. Eat foods in season. In the jungle, you only have access to food that is growing on trees or is preserved. You can research foods that are in season in your particular geographical climate. Eating foods in season provides you with the nutrients needed to survive that season.

#6. Eat beef from grass-fed cows. Eat Chicken that has not been stuffed with excess hormones to make it twice its actual size. If that's not an option for your budget, make sure it is well cooked to kill off those extra chemicals.

#7. Sleep well. Some people can function on multiple two-hour naps a day, and others need 8 hours of sleep. Be in tune with your body and stick with what works for you.

#8. Exercise well. The jungle diet requires walking, running, lifting, etc. Try to be active at work, school, and wherever you go. Don't just walk; try to power walk to burn some excess calories, increase metabolism, and keep your body's natural feel-good-hormones functioning.

To exercise naturally, you don't have to go to the gym. You can create small snippets of exercise in your typical day to day activity. For instance, instead of taking the elevator, take the stairs. Park far away from any building, so you are forced to walk. Use a shopping basket instead of a shopping cart. Use everything in your life as an opportunity to remain active.

#9. Expose yourself to the elements: water, air, and sand. The human body isn't designed to see four walls every day. Take time to look at anything natural. Observing nature's glory is incredible. All living things existing are connected.

#10. Stop counting calories; be in tune with your body instead. Counting calories is anxiety-provoking, and anxiety is not suitable for any kind of diet. It defeats the purpose of dieting. Instead of counting calories, be aware of portions. The lack of refrigeration in the jungle allows one to learn the importance of food portioning.

#11. Match your food intake with your physical activity. For instance, if you eat a bucket of fried chicken, let it match the amount of physical activity you do. Once you get to know your body, you will begin to learn to workout based on what you eat.

#12. Eat with Intention. Salads are not ideal every day. Some days, you may need more energy, and more carbs will be required to go through the day. Other days, you may need less energy. Eat according to your needs for the day. EatwithIntention

#13. Stop negative thinking. Everything starts with thoughts. If you keep worrying about being fat, it might happen. If you can envision your body the way you want it to look, and you're obeying all these rules, it'll work out.

If you want a more thorough assessment of how your current diet affects your mental health, visit a Nutritionist or a Holistic Specialist. There are specific nutrients that the body needs to help with individual mental health diagnosis.

Mental Health Savage challenge

Google foods that help with anxiety, depression, moods, etc. Buy the ingredients, cook a healthy meal, post on social media with hashtag #goodmoodgoodfood, and tell us why you chose the particular ingredients.

Be intentional with your sleep

S leep is the rejuvenation of the body and mind. Sleep allows your body to heal itself, repair muscles, and control moods. Here's the kicker. If you are struggling with depression or anxiety, you're likely sleeping too much or too little. Both are not good for your mental health.

If you are barely getting any sleep, it is important to practice healthy sleep hygiene. It goes by nine basic principles;

1. Set a fixed bedtime schedule every day. The human brain loves consistency. It loves routine. Each time you comply with a routine, things work more efficiently.
2. Create a bedtime routine to keep your body in the rhythm of sleep. If you go to bed at 10 pm, you can wake up at 7 am. It gives your nine full hours to prepare for bed and sleep. If you take a shower, shower. If you brush your teeth before bed, you have enough time to do so. The consistency gives you enough time to read for 15 minutes, journal for 10 minutes, and meditate for 5 minutes.
3. The bedroom is for sex and sleep. Pavlov created an experiment called classical conditioning. If your

brain and body knows that the bedroom is for rest and sex, each time you walk into your bedroom at the right time, you will start to feel drowsy, and if your partner is there, you will begin to feel horny. Repetition creates habits.

4. No phones, no televisions, no bright lights, and no technology. Again, back to the Jungle Diet. In the jungle, once the sun sets, the only source of light is usually a burnfire. Burn fires are somewhat dangerous because it attracts predators. So, our ancestors learned to go to bed when the sun sets and wake up when the sun rises. Phones, televisions, and other bright light sources trick our brains into thinking it is time to be awake. It is good to turn off all lights or dim the bedroom light so your body can fall asleep.

5. Wake up at the same time each day. It is all about patterns, routines, and consistency. Try to stick with it, and you'll wake up energetic.

6. Trigger your circadian rhythm when you wake up. The moment you wake up, don't try to put your alarm on snooze, get up, open the windows so the sun can come into your room, and make your bed. This forces your body to stay awake.

7. If your sleeplessness is persistent, contact your doctor to check to see if you are struggling with hyperthyroidism or other health factors that may affect your sleep patterns.

8. Nature has given us natural sleep aids like lavender and chamomile tea. You can also use essential oils to help you sleep.

9. Avoid drinking excess caffeine. Coffee lovers! After noon, start drinking water instead, to reduce the amount of caffeine in your blood.

Keep in mind that sleep, diet, and exercise are all intertwined. The body needs regularity to function. To induce sleep, working out can help. Try not to eat less than two hours before bed.

Tami Odimayo

If you are sleeping too much, you may be struggling with depression. Talk to your therapist. My general rule of thumb is to avoid taking medications for sleep until sleep hygiene practices don't work anymore.

Mental Health Savage Challenge

Take a picture of items that help with your sleep routine and use hashtag #SleepRoutine.

For example, you can take a picture of a book you read before bed, an essential oil diffuser you use, a warm bath prep method you use, etc.

Utilize the Morning Sun

Remember, Lion King? *Aaahh ti mae ya*….alright, I'll stop. There is nothing in nature as glorious as the sunrise. Darkness happens all night, and boom, the morning sun comes from nowhere. In Lion King, the sun rises, and all the animals gather to watch as Simba is technically presented as the crowned prince of the Kingdom. What does this have to do with mental health?

The sun is the source of all energy. A majority of plants need sunlight for photosynthesis. We need plants for food and to grow the animals we eat. The sun is required for the mechanical nature of the earth. When it rains, the sun dries off the earth so that the clouds can reabsorb the water, and then it rains again.

When we think of sunshine, we think about happiness. No one says, "good morning, moonlight!" For those in the mid-western or northern climates, after two months of winter and barely any sun, a majority of people begin to develop symptoms of Seasonal Depression and even the flu. Both have been linked with low levels of vitamin D, which primarily comes from the sun.

It is also not coincidental that there is a spike in suicide rates during winter months' grey skies. Our bodies thrive on the sun. That is why some of the happiest vacation spots today are places with lots and lots of sun, like Florida, California, Jamaica, Costa Rica, South Africa, etc.

But is sunlight all the way good? The answer is sometimes. Research shows that the most beneficial sunlight happens between 7 am and 10 am. After that, the sun rays may be harmful, and sunscreen is needed.

I'm not asking you to get a tan every morning. Try to wake up as early as 7 am, grab a cup of water, tea, smoothie, and drink it outside your home, while you observe the glory of nature.

One of my first jobs required me to work the graveyard shift. I was ecstatic because I was young, was already a night owl, loved that there was less work to do during the night shift, and felt like I could use most of the day to be productive. I was able to get ahead of my schoolwork, finish all the television shows I wanted to watch and had enough time to reflect on my past, present, and future.

Two weeks into working the graveyard shift, I began to feel a difference in my mood. Even when I slept nine hours during the day, I was always tired, dreaded going to work, lost interest in activities I used to enjoy, and was highly irritable. All these were classic symptoms of Depression. It took me a month to figure out what the problem was.

After my overnight shift, I would go straight to bed— missing all the essential benefits of the morning sun. By the time I would wake up, it would be roughly around late afternoon. For those who live in the winter climates, you know that the sun sets early. Sometimes, at 4 pm.

I decided to switch things up. Instead of immediately going to bed, I would go for a quick walk at a strip mall or go to the gym. I exposed myself to as much sunlight as possible. Then about noon, I would go to bed and wake up 8 hours later. I felt more energetic, could think better, and my mood began to improve.

It is all about the circadian rhythm. The human body is designed to be awake as the sun rises and asleep as the sunsets.

Simply put, maximize the benefits of the morning sun. It is not only helpful for your mental health; it is helpful for your skin, muscles, bones, and overall well-being. I love nature.

Mental Health Savage Challenge

Take a picture of yourself (selfie/photographed by another person) during the first hour of sunrise. Use hashtag #NaturesVitaminD

Workout Instinctively

I should simply say that exercise is good for the mind, body, and soul and end it like that. But how? In the year 2000, Herman and his colleagues' research demonstrated the direct influence of exercise on Major Depression. The research results showed that exercise significantly reduced the symptoms of Major Depression within four months. Another research done in 2016 showed that exercise reduced symptoms of anxiety by increasing serotonin (the feel-good neurotransmitter), reducing cortisol (the stress hormone), increasing endorphins (the neurotransmitter that reduces pain), and dopamine (reward hormone of the brain). Simply put, exercise is magic.

Here's the downside. One of the symptoms of Major Depression is fatigue or loss of energy. If you are reading this and are depressed, you probably wonder how you can gather enough energy to work out. My main suggestion is to apply the *upside-down pyramid* rule. Start small and go big.

Exercise is not just about intensity; it is about consistency. My suggestion is to create a habit of exercising. For the first thirty days, work out for thirty minutes or less at a gym or your home and do not make it overly intense, or you might dread going to the gym the next day.

1. Create a pre-workout, workout, and post-workout routine. A pre-workout routine is what you do before working out. For instance, make sure your phone is charged, create a workout playlist prior to working out to avoid looking for songs to play while at the gym and have a bottle of water. Your workout routine needs to vary per day. Make a schedule for leg day, arm day, abs, etc. Your post-workout routine should be relaxing. For instance, a bath, a shower, reading a book, watching a movie, etc.

2. For 15 minutes, walk on the treadmill or elliptical. Remember, I said walk, not run. Don't overwhelm yourself. Walk with the treadmill on high to medium incline. For the last 15 minutes, do weight-based exercises like (using dumbbells, machines, or your body weight). Several phone applications can help with this. Some gyms have free personal trainers.

3. Get a workout buddy for extra motivation.

4. Set small goals. Instead of focusing on weight loss or muscle mass gains, set goals related to how many reps or miles you can do each day. If you walked 1 mile in 15 minutes, try to walk 1.2 miles in 14 minutes the next day.

5. It is important to be okay with sweating because it releases toxins from the body.

6. Listen to calm music while you are working out. Remember that the point of exercise is to strengthen the body and relax the mind.

7. Afterward, take a cold/warm shower to help return the body's temperature to its normal state and wash the salty sweat off.

8. Don't be afraid to reward yourself.

After your 30-day trial of consistently working out, you can begin to increase the intensity and reduce the frequency.

1. Your body is now used to working out, and walking on the treadmill will be as easy as slicing an apple. You may now start to run on the treadmill or use the

mechanical staircase.

2. Instead of going daily, reduce it to every other day.
3. Try not to work out the same muscles every time. Try different muscles.
4. Appreciate your progress. It may not be ecstatically high, but it is progress. If your friend lost 20 pounds in one month, it is okay if you lost only 2 pounds. Everybody's body is different. The results you are looking for will only be seen if you are consistent.
5. After 90-days, if you suddenly stop working out, you will feel different because you have established a routine for your body.

Humans are designed to be active. Setting time aside to exercise will not only helps your neurotransmitters function better; it also helps with physical regulations like digestive health, respiratory health, cardiac health, and circulation health.

When I began private practice, I had the opportunity to work more closely with clients. A client of mine presented with intense suicidal ideation. He reported that he was generally satisfied with life. He had a good job, a good upbringing—everything seemed fine. There were no significant triggers to his symptoms. After examining his holistic lifestyle, I realized he was not eating well. When he did, it was junk food. He was not socializing outside the parameters of work, and his entire lifestyle was completely inactive. Because of this, I realized his mental health symptoms were significantly affected by his biological lifestyle.

I informed him to avoid junk food for the first thirty days, cook, and then advised him to get a gym membership. His first response was, "I don't have time." My response, "we can create time for things that matters."

An egg takes less than five minutes to fry. Vegetables take less than ten minutes to sauté. Finally, working out is only thirty minutes of your entire day. When he started working out, there was a complete change in his physical appearance. He became more energetic during sessions, his skin was better, his vibe was better, and his ability to remember core areas of his life was better. Interestingly, going to the gym regularly increased his social life because he was able to meet more people.

The bottom line is, let us go back to our true nature. Cars and machines have been created to make our lives easier. But if you can walk to the grocery store instead of driving, that counts as exercise. If you can carry your groceries in a bag instead of using the cart, that's exercise. Dance vigorously. It is an excellent workout. Exercise can be implemented in everyday lifestyle by doing the simplest things.

***Mental Health Savage Challenge ***

Post your pre-workout, workout, and post-workout routine with the hashtag #MentalHealthWorkouts feel free to screenshot your workout playlist, your workout app, your running miles, etc.

Don't forget your yearly physical assessment

#AskYourDoctor

A lot of mental health symptoms also have biological causes. For instance, high blood pressure and anxiety are closely linked. The physical illnesses you're experiencing might directly affect your mental health. For example, a client diagnosed with cancer is also struggling with Depression and Anxiety because of cancer.

Another reason why yearly physicals are beneficial is to help you know what area of your physical health to work on. Lifestyle changes can be made to address your physical health. This gives you an edge to stay on top of your physical health.

Remember that all aspects of our health are intertwined. Meaning, your physical, spiritual, mental, emotional, and relational are all working together.

Chapter 3
Your Mental Health
#MentalHealthTipsfromTami

Understand your mental Health Diagnosis

#UnderstandYourDiagnosis

In 2009, I took an abnormal psychology class. I was stunned by the number of mental illness symptoms out there. The most astonishing part of that class was that I could relate to each mental health symptom my professor taught. That was not all. I began to diagnose everyone around me silently; my parents, friends, and even professors. Interestingly, just by mere perspective, I gave almost everyone a diagnosis in my life.

I simultaneously enrolled in a Personality Disorder class and was even more surprised by the various personality traits that existed. There were some disturbing personality traits like Antisocial Personality Disorder and Sadistic Personality Disorder.

The symptoms are so general, any person reading it may think that they have a mental illness.

Depression and anxiety also seemed like a diagnosis everybody had. I realized that most people had experienced mood swings in the past. Most people have experienced feelings of sadness, lack of motivation, sudden fear or panic, sleeplessness, lack of appetite, and need to be the center of attention. Etc.

By the eighth week of class, I summoned the courage to ask my professor my mind bogging question, "Why does everyone fit one of these descriptions?" She smiled, looked directly at me, and said, *"Everyone you know will be able to fit into one of the disorders mentioned in the Diagnostic Statistical Manual. As a clinician, you're not looking at the symptoms; you're looking for the severity."*

She explained that it mainly becomes a disorder when it impairs functioning at home, school, work, or relationally. It became clear to me that each diagnosis can be turned around for a good purpose. My point is, you may experience various symptoms and not fall under the category of a Mental illness diagnosis.

When you visit a hospital, see a psychiatrist, or see mental health therapist, you might get a diagnosis recorded on file. Some of the most common diagnoses are Major Depressive Disorder and Generalized Anxiety Disorder. It is essential to ask the clinician what your diagnosis is. If you know what it is, you know what direction to go to, towards healing. If you don't understand the implications of your diagnosis, ask your clinician. Knowledge is power.

Your mental health diagnosis can be used to your benefit

This is a chapter based on my personal biases about mental health diagnosis. I believe that a mental illness diagnosis isn't a death sentence. You have an opportunity to maximize your symptoms to your benefit.

In the previous chapter, I talked about the key feature in all diagnoses. Which is, it has to impair an area of your life. This means, invariably, you may have symptoms of mental illness and choose not to let it impair your functioning by thinking about ways to use it to your advantage.

1. Bipolar Disorder

Bipolar Disorder is defined simply as extreme highs and extreme lows. An individual with bipolar disorder will experience a manic phase (inflated self-esteem, decreased need for sleep, increased risk-taking behaviors, pressured speech, racing thoughts, and increased goal-directed behavior). These traits can be highly detrimental to someone who doesn't have a healthy way to cope with them. These traits have been seen to cause impulsive criminal behaviors, excessive spending, and irrational behaviors. But, I believe, and I use this to work with my clients, that the manic phase can be managed with a rigid structural plan.

For example, a client of mine diagnosed with Bipolar Disorder came in, mostly because of his wife. He had cleaned up his bank account, created unnecessary business ideas, partied all night, and engaged in behaviors that were out of his character. My main goal was not to subdue the "manic phase" he was experiencing. Instead, I aimed to teach him how to maximize his symptoms in a healthy way. We worked on a safety plan for his next manic phase to help him manage his money. I then advised him to use his manic phase to work solely on creating a business of his interest. With counseling, support from his wife and family members, he began to use his manic phase for creativity.

The next step was to work on his depressive phase (loss of interest in activities, sleeping too much or too little, loss of appetite, decreased ability to concentrate, fatigue, etc.) Usually, when he is in this phase, he is less likely to want to leave the house. His isolation then leads to thoughts of suicide, sometimes. My goal was not to force him to leave the house. My goal was to help him maximize the depressive phase.

Interestingly, I found that his depressive symptoms allowed him to reflect inward. Naturally, I also understand that the opposite of depression is expression. Once sleep, appetite, and exercise were addressed. I began helping him focus on journaling, introspection, meditation, mindfulness, and everything that allowed him to focus on him and express himself, including utilizing support groups. Of course, I created a safety plan for potential thoughts of suicide.

Basically, my goal was to show him that his bipolar symptoms do not have to be excessively debilitating.

Attention Deficit and Hyperactivity Disorder

ADHD is one of the most commonly diagnosed disorders among children. Naturally, kids with symptoms of ADHD are recommended ADHD medications to allow them to focus in class. However, I realized that classes are not meant for everyone. Some of the kids with ADHD diagnosis that I have worked with simply have a different learning style.

Not everyone is cut out for the "standard" seat-in-class-listen-pass-your-exams.

Some kids learn by actively doing, some kids need more breaks and some kids need someone to read out each exam question. My point is, if you or anyone you know struggles with ADHD, it doesn't mean you need medications for focus. Talk to the school about getting you an IEP tailored to helping you or your child succeed better.

2. Personality Disorders

Personality disorder was one of my favorite classes in college because it introduced me to a spectrum of personality traits I was able to identify as potentially beneficial and detrimental to an individual.

For this subsection, I'll focus on three.

Narcissistic Personality Disorder

I think this is by far one of the most popular personality disorders out there. People with Narcissistic Personality Disorder have an exaggerated sense of self-importance, believe they are superior, lack empathy, take advantage of others, behave in arrogant ways, exaggerate accomplishments, have secret feelings of insecurity, have difficulty regulating emotions, etc. you get the picture. This is the characteristic of most CEOs, politicians, and lawyers. The fact of the matter is, with adequate counseling, narcissistic traits can be of benefit if toxic traits are reduced, and positive qualities are amplified.

Antisocial Personality Disorder

This is also a commonly glorified trait. Antisocial does not mean someone who doesn't want to be around others. When you think of Antisocial Personalities, think about El Chapo, Tony Soprano, Don Corleone, and Pablo Escobar. Someone with an Antisocial Personality disregards others' rights, engages in lies and deceit, callous, arrogant, manipulative, impulsive, recurrent legal problems, hostile, lack of empathy, risk-taking behaviors, failure to consider negative consequences, etc. You get the picture. The first signs of antisocial traits start before 15: violence towards people or animals, deceitfulness, destruction of property, theft, and other truant behaviors. One of the key features I noticed when I read the symptoms for the first time is that it all boils down to the lack of fear. Therefore, with adequate counseling, some of these fearless traits can benefit careers involving thrill-seeking, etc.

Histrionic Personality Disorder

Histrionic personality disorder is characterized by an excessive need for attention. This need for attention can lead to provocative dressing, impulsive behaviors, oversensitivity to criticism, rapid shift of emotions, over concern for physical appearance, difficulty maintaining relationships, low tolerance for frustration, etc. Again, this can benefit an individual by reducing the severity of the symptoms, setting goals, creating accountability, and creating positive attention-seeking behaviors.

This chapter is a work in progress. My goal is to research every single diagnosis in the DSM and find a positive outlook on it.

Prepare for Stressful situations ahead of time

S tress is an inevitable part of existence. It can either make you or break you. Because of stress, our ancestors were able to figure out more comfortable ways to function. For instance, a farmer in the 19th century had to do many physically stressful activities that a farmer in the 21st century does not have to worry about because machines were invented to make things easier. Stress breeds innovation. The problem is, a lot of people do not know how to manage stress.

Stress releases a hormone called Cortisol. Cortisol is a highly effective hormone that allows the body to control metabolism, regulate sugar levels, help with memory formation, help with adrenaline functioning, respiration, blood pressure, and so much more. See, the thing is, Cortisol isn't bad at all. However, excess release of Cortisol affects everything listed above negatively.

If a Lion walks into your bedroom, growling, Cortisol will be released, which will trigger adrenaline. With this, your body can decide to fight, flight, or freeze. This is good.

It becomes bad when your body thinks the lion is always

in the room. In this condition, your body releases excess cortisol that will then begin to disrupt metabolism, sleep difficulties, respiratory functioning, weight gain, and many more. This begins to reflect as anxiety, depression, insomnia, digestion problems, heart disease, and headaches, etc.

"If you are paying close attention, you'll realize that the above medical and mental conditions can be solved using the book's rules so far."

Simply put, stress can help the body function better if managed. If unmanaged, it makes the body function a lot worse.

So, what can be done?

Each individual has used at least one stress management coping skill in their lifetime. Coping skills to manage stress is defined as anything that can bring your body back to baseline.

For some people, it is swimming. For others, it is running. For some, it is socializing with peers. For some people, meditation, mindfulness, deep breathing, and yoga are stress reduction strategies. For others, it is finding a way to solve the source of the stress. Since stress is inevitable, everyone should have an emergency stress kit.

Many individuals don't have an instant resolution to stress. People wait for a stressor to occur before applying a coping skill. Stress coping skills can be used with or without the stressor. It is like vitamin C. You don't have to wait for your body to need vitamin C to take it. You can always take it.

Stress is like that. If swimming helps you cope with stress, swim even when you're not stressed. If running enables you to cope with stress, run even when you're not stressed.

Apply your coping skills even when you don't need

them so that the application of your coping skills become muscle memory.

When your coping skill becomes muscle memory, your body and brain will automatically seek stress reduction techniques when you are facing a stressor.

Another big mistake people make when it comes to stress reduction is the use of either legal or illegal drugs. The truth is, the use of either isn't the solution. Until you learn how to deal with stress, it will still be a problem. Drugs, medication, and alcohol only temporarily solve the symptoms, not the cause. That's why practitioners recommend both drugs and therapy to reduce medication dependency.

Mental Health Savage Challenge

Take a picture of your #EmergencyStressKit

It could be a picture of a fidget spinner, balloon for breathing, or your journal and make a post with the above hashtag.

Process every instance of grief, loss, or trauma

Trauma is a seed. It happens to everybody. It is painful for some, and it can be painless for others. Regardless, trauma is trauma. If it is unmanaged, that seed begins to build and grow. Eventually, it becomes an annoying tree that affects every branch of your life; relational, mental, emotional, physical, and spiritual health.

The weird thing about trauma is, sometimes you're unaware that you have been traumatized—this is what we call the unconscious.

What is trauma?

Trauma is anything that has a psychological impact on you regardless of your awareness of it. Trauma can be a single occurrence or recurrent. Trauma is experiencing the sudden death of a loved one, a physical accident, abuse, experiencing military combat exposure, unwanted sexual advances, neglect from a caregiver, sudden loss of employment, sudden break-up, witnessing another person in pain, exposure to argumentative parents, recurrent rejection, exposure to animal cruelty, early exposure to violent crimes, etc.

Anything can trigger a traumatic response. It all depends on the individual and society. For instance, if you grew up in a war zone, seeing someone shot to death might not create a traumatic response because you're used to it. However, if you didn't grow up in a war zone, and you witness someone shot to death in plain sight, you might begin to have post-traumatic responses.

According to the book, *the boy who was raised by a Dog*, by Doctor Bruce Perry, the entire human body experiences trauma. Soldiers who come back from their respective deployments sometimes experience these traumatic re-enactments at all parts of their body. For instance, a combat veteran I worked with has reported feeling pain in his leg, years after he was shot. If it was a persistent pain, it would be understandable. However, his pain gets triggered during the Fourth of July fireworks. Another client I worked with reported that she still feels her abuser on top of her, years after her stepfather molested her.

A client of mine, Jane (for confidentiality reasons), came to counseling because she couldn't sleep at night. Due to the lack of sleep, other mental health symptoms began to present itself. She became more and more depressed, her anxiety levels were at an all-time high, and because of this, she couldn't focus at work and was irritable with people. My main goal was to make sure she slept because sleep, diet, and exercise need to be met to make bigger goals more achievable. After those goals were met, I began to process and explore her entire life with her.

She was sure that she hadn't experienced any emotional, physical, psychological, or sexual trauma. She reported, "I just can't sleep." I processed and explored her lifestyle, what she ate, what she drank, the amount of exercise she had, the drugs she had used in the past, etc. Everything seemed fine. She wasn't highly caffeinated. She didn't use "upper" drugs, she ate at the right time, and though she didn't exercise, her job was physically exerting enough. She identified that she had running thoughts, but nothing recurrent. After three sessions, she recognized that her sleeplessness happened around the same time every year—the fall season. When I asked if anything significant happened in the fall, years ago, she said the only thing she remembered was being raided by the police.

Three years before our first session, she began dating a guy. She didn't know he was a drug dealer. Right in the middle of the night, she heard a loud bang on the door. The police barged in, pinned her boyfriend to the floor, and searched the entire apartment for what felt like hours. While this was happening, she was also thoroughly searched and rough-handled. They found drugs. She identified that she broke up with him and moved on from it, "It didn't affect me."

Interestingly, ever since, around the same time, she would be up all night because her body remembered. She processed her trauma over and over again until it had no power. Her awareness of the problem made it easier for her to deal with it. Her sleep improved, and eventually, every area of her life also improved.

Trauma has power when it is a secret that's not dealt with.

Trauma cannot be ignored. It always finds a way to express itself later on in life.

For instance, another client of mine, *John Doe, got into a car accident. He was prescribed pain pills and soon became addicted to pain pills. Eventually, he lost everything because his addiction switched from pain pills to Heroin (which is common in today's opiate crisis). He lost his job, family, and eventually began to spend more time in jail. On the surface level, it looked like John's addiction was based solely on his accident.*

After spending some time working with him, I realized that the prescribed pain pills became an escape from his traumatic childhood. A neighbor molested him before he was a teenager. He kept that secret for so long he was unaware of the psychological impact on him. By the time he became aware of its impact, he was already physically and psychologically dependent on his pills. He was referred to an expert trauma counselor who applied EMDR (Eye movement desensitization and reprocessing), which helped him work on his trauma. His life continues to show progress.

Trauma is heavy baggage that doesn't discriminate based on race or gender. The important thing to remember is, **"You are not your trauma." Your traumatic experience wasn't your choice, but your healing is.**

Mental Health Savage Challenge

Share a message of empowerment to your followers. P.S it is not recommended that you share your trauma to your followers. Just a message of empowerment. #FaceYourTrauma

Be aware of emotional and psychological triggers

Awareness is difficult in today's environment. On a typical day, we are swamped with thousands of distractions—things I have tagged as unnecessary stimuli. These excessive stimuli make it difficult for us to identify what affects our emotions negatively. Lao Tzu said, "The key to growth is the introduction of higher dimensions of consciousness into our awareness."

Humanity never takes action to solve a problem until awareness comes into place. Freud, the father of psychology, spent his entire life talking about the "unconscious" and bringing the unconscious to the conscious. For the most part, we run on autopilot on a day to day basis, and the body loves that.

For instance,

How many times have you driven to work and not remember anything in between?

How many times have you turned on the TV to watch a movie and you don't remember the last twenty minutes of the movie?

55

Tami Odimayo

How many times have you sat in on a conversation and realized that your mind had been elsewhere?

If I asked you to tell me what the last person you spoke to was wearing, will you be able to tell me?

The human mind is designed to absorb details. Unfortunately, a majority of the details don't get transferred to our conscious working memory. When I run group therapy, I sometimes ask clients to close their eyes and name twenty-five objects around them or describe it. Eight times out of ten, the client I chose would not name more than ten items.

This becomes trickier when dealing with mental health and substance abuse. We face triggers daily. A smell might trigger anger. The sound of an object might trigger PTSD flashbacks. Someone's comment might trigger depressive thoughts, and the way someone grabs you might lead to an explosion like no other.

I came across a client whose trigger was a word I cannot comfortably type in this book. You could call him any bad name known to humanity, and he won't get upset, but this particular word caused a violent anger outburst. It turns out that his uncle used to use that word before physically abusing him.

I have found that many people aren't aware of their emotional triggers, and it is because of one keyword, "Mindfulness." Mindfulness is the ability to remain in the present. Mindfulness is how you can learn to identify your emotional and psychological triggers.

Read the Mindfulness chapter for more information.

Mental Health Savage Challenge

Name a trigger you have discovered recently and share using #DiscoverYourTrigger

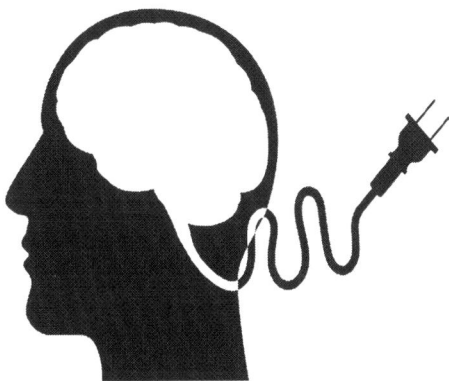

Chapter 4
Addiction, Medications, and Substances

#NaturalHappiness

Don't substitute substances for healing

This chapter is mostly for individuals who self-medicate with drugs, alcohol, and even prescribed medications. Substances are not meant to be the end-all healing virtue. There is no magic pill that can last forever. Eventually, our bodies begin to build tolerance for medications, drugs, and alcohol. So, when the substances wear out of our system, the problem is still there.

For instance, if you are dealing with anxiety by smoking some weed. Yes, the weed helps, but what are you doing to address the source of anxiety?

I have seen many individuals cope with a stressful situation for years by substituting the healing, using substances, and then waking up to realize that they have lived in an unhealthy situation for that long because they have been coping in a harmful way.

Using a substance without dealing with the problem will only allow you to live in the problem for longer than you need to.

What's even worse, I know individuals who still don't realize that the job or relationship they have is unhealthy for their spirit, soul, and body. The alcohol they continue to drink to manage the stress has clouded their judgment.

For the sake of your mental health, don't utilize any substance to manage mental health stressors. Continuing to do so will cause your brain to associate, "I am angry" with "I need a drink" or "I am anxious" with, "I need to smoke a blunt," or I have a pill to manage this or that. Deal with the problem first before or while considering any form of medication or substance.

Mental Health Savage Challenge

What's a problem you have been avoiding for a long time? What have you done to avoid the problem? What can you do to face the problem? #TrueHealing

Explore natural remedies for mental health

#NaturalHappiness

Mental illnesses have a variety of treatment options. As said in previous chapters, I believe that nature has given us everything that we need to survive as a species. It is left for us to discover it. In recent times, alternative natural remedies have been found to help with mental health. One of the most famous natural herbs people use is the jack of all trades, Marijuana.

Researchers from far and wide have studied marijuana's effect on anxiety, pain, fibromyalgia, anorexia, depression, and even ADHD. They have determined that marijuana has a positive impact on reducing the effects of some mental illnesses. Here's the catch. Although marijuana has some fantastic results, it has a high potential for abuse if misused.

Before I continue this chapter, I would like to state that I am not endorsed by any natural remedy company. I'm not a medical doctor, and you should consult with your Medical Doctor and or Psychiatrist before trying any of these remedies. Also, remember that using natural remedies isn't the only thing you need to use. You'll need to work on all core areas that influence your mental health (spiritual, emotional, physical, psychological, and relational). Seeing a Therapist will always be beneficial. Lastly, just because it is natural doesn't mean it is safe at all doses. Consult with a specialist.

That being said, according to Medical News Today, these are some natural supplements that can help with mental health symptoms;

1. St John's Worth: this natural supplement can be used to combat depression. However, if you're going through severe major depression, please talk to your psychiatrist first.
2. Ginseng: this is a natural Asian remedy that has been said to improve memory by providing mental clarity, increasing energy, and reducing stress.
3. Chamomile: this natural supplement can be used for insomnia. It is available in tea form at most stores— commonly known as *sleepy time tea.* It can also be used for anxiety and depression.
4. Lavender: Lavender essential oils can be used to induce sleep and reduce anxiety. It promotes relaxation and helps with moods.
5. Omega 3 fats: Can be found in fish and fish oil. This helps boost brainpower.
6. Valerian root: sounds like a Game of Thrones herb. This can help with anxiety.
7. Kava: this natural substance is commonly used in South Asia pacific areas to boost mood, relieve stress, and provide calmness.

Natural remedies are not limited to substances. Music therapy, exercise, yoga, mindfulness, meditation, and progressive muscle relaxation are all-natural ways to alleviate mental health symptoms.

Mental Health Savage Challenge

Take a picture of yourself doing something natural that makes you happy #NaturalHappiness.

Understand every substance you ingest

I asked a friend of mine to tell me three potential health benefits of drinking alcohol and three dangers of drinking alcohol. He could not tell me. My question was, "then why are you drinking alcohol?"

I'm not against alcohol or any other substance. I'm against the lack of knowledge associated with substance use. According to the National Institute of Drug Abuse, more than fifty percent of Heroin users began with prescribed pain pills like Oxytocin, Vicodin, etc. It is a startling number. Another shocking statistic is that 1 in 4 individuals who are currently struggling with addiction began before 18.

Based on these statistics, two things are clear;

1. Just because a Medical Doctor prescribed it doesn't mean the drug is right for you.
2. Most addicts didn't fully know the substance they were taking when they started taking it.

That being said, what should you know before taking any substance?

a. Is this substance addictive?

This is one of the core factors you should check for. Most illegal drugs, like cocaine, inhalants, methamphetamine, heroin, fentanyl, are highly addictive. Legal drugs, like benzodiazepines, prescribed opiates, and amphetamines, have addictive qualities. There are alternatives to all of them.

b. Does anyone in my family have a history of addiction?

If you have a family member (parent, uncle, sister, grandparents, etc.) that struggles with addiction, drinking, or using drugs, isn't the best idea. Like many mental illnesses, the genetic nature of addiction has been questioned. A child of an alcoholic has a higher chance of becoming an alcoholic.

c. Do the potential benefits outweigh the risk?

If you have watched a drug ad on television, you would know that some medications have scary side effects. If your doctor prescribes you a medication, ask about ALL potential risks. If the risks are heavy, find a way to counteract the risks. For instance, a client who was prescribed an antidepressant increased her workouts to prevent weight gain.

If you are thinking about using illicit substances, think about the addictive properties, legal issues you may face, and potential damage to significant parts of your body's organs.

d. Are there natural alternatives?

I believe Nature has given us everything we need to survive. There are natural alternatives for every medication. Ask your Doctor about Holistic measures. First, ask yourself what your goal is, and look for what substance provides that goal. For instance, an alternative for benzodiazepine could be CBD oils.

Okay, so when writing this chapter, I decided to give a quick cheat sheet on illicit substances, the adverse side effects, and positive side effects.

Alcohol

Drinking Alcohol is not necessarily a bad thing. After all, Jesus turned water into wine. Here's where it gets tricky. According to the National Institute of Drug Abuse, Alcohol has been the most dangerous substance on earth due to the ease of access, legal costs, societal costs, medical costs, and relational costs. Withdrawing from alcohol without medical assistance can lead to seizures and death. The effects of alcohol vary from person to person and are determined by age, family health history, and amount used. Alcohol affects the heart, liver, brain, and pancreas. It also weakens the immune system. Isn't it weird that a simple drink could cause this much damage?

Yep. As a Substance Abuse Counselor, I worry about clients who struggle with alcohol the most because alcohol isn't something you can simply avoid seeing. It is at grocery stores, gas stations, restaurants—everywhere. I noticed that people who use alcohol to self-medicate or cope with a stressor are more likely to become addicted. For instance, if you drink anytime you are upset, can't sleep, anxious, etc., your body will learn to depend on alcohol when you feel those feelings.

The bottom line is if you are going to drink, drink in moderation. You don't have to get blackout drunk to have fun. If anyone in your family is an alcoholic, drinking should be done with extreme caution, preferably, not at all.

Cocaine

Cocaine is one of the most famous party drugs. It exists in powdered form and rock form (crack). Cocaine's lethality can cause narrowed blood vessels, enlarged pupils, increased body temperature, heart rate, and blood pressure; headache, abdominal pain, and nausea, euphoria, increased energy, alertness, insomnia, restlessness, anxiety, erratic and violent behavior, panic attacks, paranoia, psychosis, heart rhythm problems, heart attack; stroke, seizure, coma. The withdrawal symptoms aren't fun either; depression, tiredness, increased appetite, insomnia, vivid, unpleasant dreams, slowed thinking and movement, restlessness. Cocaine is a tricky drug because you may get the worst symptoms without experiencing any of the good. Some people can use cocaine and not get addicted, and others will try it and be addicted immediately.

Opiates

Opiates are one of the most underestimated drugs I know. Most people who experience intense physical accidents are prescribed opiates. It is easily addictive because of the euphoric effects. Opiates could be prescribed by a Doctor or could be gotten on the streets in Heroin form.

According to NIDA, the withdrawals from Opiates are intense, and addicts report continued use to avoid the sickness that comes with suddenly stopping. The common effects of opiates are euphoria, dry mouth, itching, nausea, vomiting, analgesia, slowed breathing, and heart rate. When switching to the Heroin form, it becomes even more lethal Collapsed veins; abscesses (swollen tissue with pus); infection of the lining and valves in the heart; constipation and stomach cramps; liver or kidney disease; pneumonia.

The Opiate pandemic has caused a lot of Overdoses and Deaths. If you're reading this and you're addicted to Opiates, remember that there is Hope. Call your local rehab. Medical and therapeutic options are available to reduce the withdrawals' intensity and help you abstain from use.

Methamphetamine

The first time I heard about Methamphetamine, commonly known as Meth or Ice, was the TV Show, Breaking Bad. It seemed like an exciting drug, but it isn't. Meth has the most dopamine release in the brain, which makes it more addictive. The problem with Meth is that almost anyone can make it. Hence, making it one of the most lucrative options for those living in small towns. The problem with Meth is that it makes individuals feel more productive because of the lack of need for sleep and sometimes, the ability to focus. Long term Meth use can lead to anxiety, confusion, insomnia, mood problems, violent behavior, paranoia, hallucinations, delusions, weight loss, severe dental problems ("meth mouth"), intense itching leading to skin sores from scratching, according to NIDA. Most individuals who use meth heavily develop profound hallucinations that may affect the brain, long term. If someone offers you Meth, run.

Marijuana

Contrary to popular belief, marijuana is addictive and has adverse side effects also. One of the most common negative side effects of marijuana is its ability to trigger schizophrenic symptoms in those predisposed to it. According to NIDA, Marijuana causes enhanced sensory perception and euphoria followed by drowsiness/relaxation, slowed reaction time, problems with balance and coordination, increased heart rate and appetite, problems with learning and memory, anxiety. Does marijuana have health benefits? Absolutely, but so does every drug known to humanity. And like every drug, Marijuana can be abused.

If you want to use marijuana for health reasons, remember that it is okay, but remember that it has a high potential for abuse. Please use it as prescribed. Smoking joints every hour on the hour will lead to dependency.

Know your body before putting any substance in it.

Mental Health Savage Challenge

Share your most current knowledge about a medication or drug you have used. Talk about the benefits and side effects. Use hashtag #IfYouUseItKnowIt

Chapter 5
Your Support System

#MySupportTribe

Examine your relationship with your parents

In my first Psychology class, Introduction to Psychology, I learned about a man called Sigmund Freud. Freud can simply be described as weird, especially when he wrote about the Oedipus Complex. For those who don't know, the Oedipus complex happens when a son desires to hurt his father or is jealous of his father because he is sexually attracted to his mother. This principle goes for daughters towards their opposite-sex parent, also. Yes, weird—very weird. I could not understand why this man believed what he believed or why he wrote a book about it. The very first thing that came to my mind was, "Who is his mother?" urgh, never mind.

That being said, I had to open my mind to Freud's Oedipus complex. The very first relationship we develop, post-birth, is a relationship with our mothers. In some cases, fathers, but mostly mothers. We innately learn to bond with our parents because that is our survival basis for food, shelter, and water.

It doesn't end there.

We learn from our parents. Our parents show us what behaviors are acceptable and unacceptable. Our sense of morality, understanding of love, and communication styles, usually come from our parents. Mostly, how we deal with mental health stressors is sometimes learned from our parents.

Our parent's behaviors do not necessarily mean that we have to develop those same behaviors. Still, we adopt a lot of our parent's actions "unconsciously."

I once worked with two teenage brothers. Due to confidentiality, I'll call them John and Jake. Both John and Jake grew up with a severely abusive father, who would not only beat them up but beat up their mother, also.

Kids who grow up in abusive households go through extreme anxiety because of fear of the unknown. The unpredictability of mom or dad's rampage is enough to cause long term psychological discomfort.

Will Mom be happy today? Or will Dad come back home drunk and angry? This kind of uncertainty leaves children in a constant flight or fight state.

The flight or fight response is our natural way to survive. If I see a lion, I would either fight the lion or run away from the lion. In some cases, I may freeze. The adrenaline that occurs when I see the lion is good for the thirty minutes I need to respond to the lion. However, if my adrenaline is still activated for the next three hours, five hours, or even weeks, I would eventually deplete my energy because the body isn't designed to be in that state for too long. This state is known as Adrenal fatigue or dysregulation.

Simply put, these brothers experienced being in a constant flight or fight state every day, for years. Jake became precisely like his father. He became a bully, loved to intimidate others, loved inflicting pain on others, and was very aggressive. John was the opposite. John became a nurturer. John learned to stand up to bullies. He learned to take care of his mother after a domestic violence incidence.

My point is, both brothers were influenced by their relationship with their parents. One chose a good path, and the other chose a completely different path. One was sent to a behavioral school, and the other had an almost perfect behavioral record at school.

Nature versus Nurture

It does not stop there. The behaviors we observe from our parents during childhood is only the tip of the iceberg. There's more. For decades, Psychologists have debated Nature versus Nurture. They have run several social experiments to test if we are primarily inclined to act based on our genes or based on learned environmental behaviors. In the case of John and Jake, did Jake inherit his father's aggressive temperament genetically, or did he just learn that such actions are acceptable?

The truth is, I don't know. As a Therapist, it is clear that both nature and nurture have a part to play—equally. John, the well-behaved child, began to suffer from the same addiction to alcohol his father suffered from, then began to struggle with the same depressive symptoms his mother had later in life.

This is why I believe it is essential to examine your relationship with your parents. If you work into most mental health facilities, counseling agencies, or hospitals, they almost always ask about your family's history of mental health. It is important to know this for diagnostic purposes and treatment purposes. For instance, if multiple members of my family were diagnosed with schizophrenia, there's a chance that I may experience schizophrenic symptoms at some point in my lifetime.

Being aware of your parents and your parent's family history is essential in understanding your mental health and ways to cope. Talk to your parents or someone who knows all family members. #TalkToYourParents

Resentments

A lot of clients I see have processed resentments they have towards their parents. It is safe to say that some of us are inclined towards resenting our parents because of physical, mental, emotional, and sometimes sexual trauma inflicted by a parent. The resentment could be because of something less severe;

"My father was never home."

"My mother was overprotective or smothering."

"I never met my father."

"My mother would neglect us at home while she's with her various boyfriends."

"My parents didn't give me the kind of love I wanted."

"I was always scared at home."

Whatever the resentment may be, it is important to work through it, because unresolved resentments towards a parent sip into adulthood. It affects your relationship with people who remind you of them. It affects how you pick romantic relationships. It affects what you can or cannot tolerate relationships. In some cases, it triggers post-traumatic stress symptoms.

For instance, Jake is dating someone who reminds him of his mother. Through counseling, I have been able to help him understand that he picks passive women that he can easily intimidate. Ironically, he hates that his girlfriend is like his mother. Still, he acts like his father towards his girlfriend. John, his brother, has also found that he naturally gravitates towards women who need his "protection." The women he unconsciously picks have struggled with an abusive relationship in the past, need a lot of emotional support, and are passive. Though he is not like his father, he tends to do anything to please her, at his own emotional and mental expense.

It is important to work on forgiveness and acceptance. Forgiveness does not mean you need to continue to expose yourself to the same negativity you experienced in childhood. A phone call or face to face meeting with a parent you are resentful towards might help. You may get closure, and you may not. Either way, practice acceptance. Some things are out of your control, and some people may never change.

Simply put, process the emotional resentments you have towards your parent with a Therapist before getting or committing into any serious relationship. If you don't, you're likely to bring heavy childhood baggage into your relationships because hurt people hurt people.

Mental Health Savage challenge

Draw a family tree and markdown significant patterns. For instance, who had a mental illness? Who struggled with addiction? Who was divorced? Who was the extrovert or introvert? There are unlimited patterns you can find in your family tree. #FamilyTree

Actively create and maintain a support network

#MySupportTribe

I worked at an outpatient substance abuse facility for two years. One of the things we always told clients was to change people, places, and things. Every successful recovering addict knows that connections matter—the people you spend time with matter—the environment you spend time in matters. I learned that maintaining a support network is beneficial to every area of mental health recovery.

Since birth, we have relied on connection to a person. As a matter of fact, since fertilization in the womb, we have relied on a connection. Research shows that a lot of experiences mothers have during pregnancy could affect the baby. If your mother was exposed to violence during her pregnancy with you, it might affect your reaction to violence in childhood and adulthood.

The connections we make after birth also ensures our survival. We build bonds with siblings, classmates, extended family members, coworkers, and, eventually, relationships. The bonds we make help us grow or weakens us.

Recent research shows that loneliness is one of the biggest epidemics out there. People are beginning to have fewer close friends. Also, with the rise of social media, people tend to confuse quantity with quality. For instance, I can have one hundred friends on Facebook and have no true friends.

A friend is someone you can confide in and achieve full emotional vulnerability. Unfortunately, a lot of people don't ever reach that level of friendship. Men! We are more guilty of this than our female counterparts.

It is time to end superficial intimacy and work on genuine intimacy. What are the things you are afraid people may know about you? Why do you wear a mask to show that you're okay in front of others? How will you feel if a living human knew everything about you? Better or worse?

These are the questions you should ask yourself daily. How many people can you call when you are feeling depressed or angry? How many people in your life understand how to calm you down? How many people can you call when you need to get bailed out?

I tell my clients to build an army of support. If you have twenty friends or acquaintances (this could include family members too), at least one of them will pick up when you need someone to vent to. Keep in mind that quantity doesn't always matter. Quality matters, as well. I could have 20 unreliable friends, and you could have five reliable friends.

Find people you can rely on. Don't settle.

The golden rule is to treat others the way you want to be treated. Be the friend that you want. Be the family that you want. When you do this, you are teaching people how you want to be treated. If the people around you aren't treating you the way you want to be treated, it is time to find a new support system.

You shouldn't have to question your support system. Your support system will call you to check on you even if you don't call to check-in. Your support system will recognize signs and patterns of your mental illness and can help.

Your support system is most likely going to be interested in the same hobbies you are interested in. For instance, if you like to golf, play basketball, and volunteer, you might have someone in your support network who does all three or have three individuals for each of those activities.

Picture your support system as roots. They keep you firm through storms and sunshine. They strengthen you. They don't pull you down. That's your true support system.

Remember, as said in earlier chapters, you have to be yourself to identify and attract the right people into your life.

Mental Health Savage Challenge

Take a picture of you and your support tribe.

Seek true human connection

Human beings are built to connect. Our survival is based on how we interact with those in our environment. Our very first connection is usually with a parent or caregiver. We learned to cry until we got help. We learned to laugh with others. We learned ways to be polite.

Connection is everything. If you are sick and you want to see a Doctor, you need to socialize. If you are hungry and want to eat at a restaurant or buy groceries, you will need socialization to order or pay for food. At school, socialization is essential. At work, socialization is essential. Everywhere you go, socialization is required. But the big question is, what is the difference between socialization and connection?

Socialization is necessary. We have to talk to the cash register. We have to interact with some of our co-workers. We might need to interact with family members or friends for drinks, gatherings, parties, etc.

However, connection is different. Connection gives life to our being.

Okay, let's rewind. Back in the day, during the pre-technology era, we were forced to form bonds with our family friends. Instead of scrolling through pictures on Instagram and Facebook, we would sit by a campfire and talk about our day for hours. When I was thinking about this, I asked myself, "What did they talk about, and how were they able to continue a conversation for hours?" I don't know, because I didn't grow up in that era.

However, I remember my childhood before I got my first phone. My friends and I would play, laugh, joke around, get in trouble together, laugh some more about that one time we played a prank on someone, play, talk some more, and the cycle continued. I knew my best friend's favorite color, favorite pair of shoes, insecurities, favorite toys, favorite movies—you get the picture. Because of the absence of social media, we were able to connect on a deeper level.

Social media has made it a lot easier to connect and find out all the information you want to know about a potential friend, without asking them directly. You can find a person's job, relationship status, favorite color, interests, etc. by just clicking the "about me" section on Facebook. We can know more in a click, so we are connecting less.

The quality of friendships has changed ecstatically. In recent research, scientists have discovered that the number of close friends an average individual will have in their lifetime has slowly declined in the past 40 years. Due to work and other demands of life, people chose to connect via social media.

For example, in a given week, besides my co-workers and some family members, I physically spend time with a friend, once, on a Friday night or Saturday night, twice a month. I mean, this is good for today's generation, but is it good enough?

My colleague once shared to me that a person can be surrounded by people but still be lonely. That statement hit me hard. I did my research and realized that the concept of Loneliness isn't new. Loneliness is linked to several physical and mental health disorders like anxiety and high blood pressure.

When I added this to one of the Mental Health rules, I had to ask myself what genuine human connection was. If one is trying to avoid being lonely, how can one connect with another human being? Is it about being able to share deep intimate secrets with another human being? Or is it simply about being free enough to be your true self around someone? Then I asked myself, why can't it be both? Why can't we define "true human connection" the way we want.

Most of my clients have a limited positive support system. I slowly began to realize that the kind of friends we have determines who we are. For instance, when working with clients suffering from addiction, I realized two things;

1. Dysfunctional family upbringing. In some cases, parents were also Addicts who neglected them. Over time they learned that to cope with life stressors, instead of talking about this with others, it was easier to bond with a drink, needle, or smoke pipe.
2. Most of my client's close friends were also in active addiction or toxic.

My job as a Therapist is to help clients reconstruct their support system. Invariably, I recommend going to Alcoholics Anonymous or Narcotic Anonymous meetings to grow their support network and gain a sponsor. These kinds of support groups give an individual someone to talk to about deep mental, relational, emotional, and spiritual stressors. I have examined all successful recovery addicts. The common denominator was a positive support network.

If this could work for addiction, how about other mental health diagnoses? It felt like a breakthrough even though most Therapists knew about this already. The next question is, how do you know who is good enough to connect with?

I came across a Tyler Perry video. He related our lives to

a tree.

You will meet a lot of people in your life.

Some people are leaves. These people are meant to be in your life for a season. They will beautify your tree. Once their job is done, in your life, they fall off. Leaves waiver from place to place and can fall off with the slightest wind. True friends and genuine connections will be undisturbed by adverse conditions.

Some people are branches. Branches also help with beautifying your tree. However, branches are not meant to be in your life forever. They provide stability, but not for long. Eventually, they break off your tree.

Some people are roots. Roots are meant to be in your life forever. Roots supply nourishment to your tree. They keep you stable. If you cut off a tree, your tree will still grow as long as the roots exist.

Some people are holding on to leaves that are not providing any benefit to their tree. If a dead leaf remains on a plant, it sucks nutrients out from the other parts of the tree. When it is time to let go of a connection, your body will know.

To find a genuine connection, follow these basic principles;

1. Be yourself. If you pretend to be someone else, you're going to attract someone attracted to the version you have created for others to see.
2. Follow your instincts. If you feel like you might not be able to trust someone, you're probably right. Building connections take work but shouldn't cause excess anxiety.
3. Live with intention. Ask yourself what this new friend brings to the picture. Is this person going to move you towards your purpose or away from your purpose? Your friends and family should help you grow

spiritually, mentally, physically, and emotionally. If they are hindering your growth, consistently, this may sound harsh, but they've got to go.

4. Be vulnerable. Vulnerability is scary but is necessary for building a connection. Based on my observation, most women have more in-depth conversations about their insecurities than men. This helps women have more intimate friendships. This part is also essential because you want an army of loyal friends who can help you cope with your day to day stressors.

5. Keep in touch by doing hobbies together.

Create a support tribe that works for you.

Mental Health Savage Challenge

Take a picture of your support system using hashtag #SupportTribe

Understand yourself before getting into a romantic relationship

#UnderstandYourself

Romance is great. We have been taught the blessings of romance since childhood. Disney and other animation companies embed this into every movie and TV show. Because of this, we consciously and unconsciously seek love and affection. To enjoy the benefit of romance, certain things have to be dealt with first.

If you get chickenpox and spend time hugging everyone you meet at the mall, at school, at work, and at home, there would be a chickenpox outbreak in your city. If you had coronavirus and spent enough time sneezing everywhere you go, there'd be a lot of people having the coronavirus in two weeks.

Doctors and the Centers for Disease and Control take epidemics like these seriously. If they have to isolate one person for thirty days to save a whole town, they would. If they have to quarantine an entire city, they will. Contagious diseases spread and spread fast.

Mental health is similar. Many people carry heavy loads of trauma, self-esteem issues, resentments towards a parent, addiction, and other unmanaged mental health stressors. In some cases, getting into a relationship before healing from all these may seem like a coping skill, but it is not. Unresolved mental health stressors always affect our relationships. And you noticed I said, "always." That's right always.

There are two types of people: people who move towards self-discovery and self-actualization before getting into a serious/committed relationship and people who move towards a direction of self-discovery while in a relationship. There's nothing wrong with either, but the second option is guaranteed to lead to resentments.

Not dealing with your emotional stressors can lead to many dissonances because, as you discover yourself, you may find that your partner isn't what you want. This will lead to a series of monogamous relationships or, worse, infidelity.

In my years of working as a counselor, I have never met an individual with an unresolved mental health stressor who is in a healthy relationship with their partner.

Now, you may be thinking, what is healthy and what is unhealthy?

A healthy relationship is a relationship where both parties can be the version of themselves that allows the relationship to grow in a healthy manner.

In simple terms, a healthy relationship is a relationship where both parties have reached self-actualization. However, it is impossible to reach self-actualization when you cannot identify what makes you who you are.

This is where counseling and mental health treatment comes in. It explores how the past may have affected your view of the present and the future.

For instance, there's a gentleman I worked with. For the sake of confidentiality, I will call him Douglas. Douglas is a successful Director, with a lovely house, two dogs, two kids, and a wife. On the outside, he has a perfect life. Everyone seemed to want to have what he has. On the inside, their marriage was as toxic as toxic can be. Douglas has dealt with depression all his life. His depression switched into an unhealthy dose of Narcissism. While exploring Douglas' past, it was clear that he held many resentments towards his mother for the physical and emotional abuse she perpetrated on him. Like I said, looking from the outside, Douglas didn't show any stereotypical signs of depression besides day to day irritability and agitation. Douglas' wife was from a healthy household. She had not experienced any noticeable trauma and was an all-round loveable human. Doug became as spiteful and vindictive as his mother. Over time, his behaviors towards his wife forced her into a state of depression, anxiety. It created a never-ending cycle of toxicity.

Am I blaming Doug for triggering depressive symptoms in his wife? Of course not. Doug is just an all-round loveable human as well. He just fell under the rot of not allowing himself to heal before marriage. Once Doug understood the generational cycle of dysfunction from his family, and once he learned how to cope with his depression symptoms, his marriage began to improve as well.

Unaddressed mental illness will always affect your significant other in one way or the other. If you are already in a relationship, I'm not recommending that you leave. I recommend working together to heal on the mental and emotional level, so other areas of your life will not be affected.

Another suggestion is that when you leave an unhealthy relationship, work on processing it with a counselor or trusted one before getting into another relationship because you may bring the baggage from one relationship to the next.

For confidentiality reasons, *I'll call this client of mine, Jane. Jane had been sexually abused by her stepfather several times when she was a child. When she told her mother, her mother didn't believe her.*

Her mother was a chronic alcoholic. She had a habit of drinking until she passed out. When her mother woke up, everything was fine; her stepfather was either in bed or cooking breakfast for the entire house. It was difficult for her mother to believe that her stepfather would do such a thing. Jane's mother suffered from low self-esteem. She was afraid to leave her husband because she felt no one else would want her. Because of her mother's low self-esteem, her stepfather had a free reign to be emotionally, physically, and mentally abusive, without fear of any repercussions.

Jane has been in multiple unhealthy relationships since she was 15 years old. In her current relationship, sometimes, while having sex, she'd push him away. The "simplest things" triggered an emotional outburst. This has caused her to lose a lot of relationships and sometimes caused domestic violence from her partner. Here is where things go south. Jane had never sought counseling for the trauma. She had buried her past and never dealt with it. Unfortunately, the more she buried it, the more she became like her mother. She began drinking to cope and her self-esteem slowly diminished. When she came for counseling, she became aware of how her trauma was causing a cyclical pattern. During the process, she discovered that her mother was also abused when she was a child.

To break the cycle, Jane began a scary journey of self-discovery. In sessions, she began to identify what triggers her emotional outbursts. She found out that something as simple as the smell of her fiancé's shaving cream was a trigger. She was able to process her trauma, stop drinking, discover her coping skills, and eventually discover herself. She left her fiancé and began to seek ways to embrace her true self. She realized that she was picking men who reminded her of her stepfather. Even if they were not like him, they became like him because she reflected her trauma on them. When she found herself, she began to attract healthier relationships.

The bottom line is, no matter how hard we try, our past influences our present. If you don't love yourself, how do you want to love? How can you identify what you can or cannot tolerate in a relationship? How can you identify how to react to things you cannot tolerate?

The journey towards self-discovery will have ups and downs. Pay attention to the patterns of your life. Repeating the same mistake over and over again is inevitable if you are not dealing with the "thing" that has to be dealt with.

A famous saying goes, "If you don't heal your wounds, you will bleed all over those you love." Work on healing first to understand what you can or cannot tolerate when you meet the one.

Mental Health Savage Challenge

What have you discovered about yourself this past month? Make a post using #UnderstandYourself

P.S., please make sure you are comfortable with posting before you do.

Sex

Sex is a crucial part of our existence. It is part of our survival. It is not something to be afraid or ashamed of, it is something to honor and enjoy. Sex can be highly beneficial in reducing anxiety, blood pressure, depression, sleeplessness, and pain.

Sex is a natural anti-depressant and anti-anxiety medication. Sex releases dopamine (essential for motivation, feelings of happiness), endorphins (reduces pain and stress), and oxytocin (increases feelings of closeness with someone else).

Sex is exercise. It is the most natural exercise. It is one of the easiest ways to burn calories if done the right way.

However, here's the problem. Sex with the wrong person can cause the opposite effect. Sex in a toxic relationship can lead to intense feelings of anxiety and depression.

Sex is energy. Spiritually and physically, sex is a transfer of energy. Emotionally, it is a way to increase intimacy and bonding. Because of this, sex can cloud your judgment when it comes to leaving an emotionally toxic relationship.

For instance, from time to time, I have a client who is in a toxic relationship and is working towards leaving. One of the very first things I recommend is stopping the act of sex. Because sex is literally like a drug, stopping will feel like withdrawal. In most cases, I find that eliminating the act of sex allows you to see your romantic relationship with a different pair of emotional glasses. Once you can see clearly, you can make much better decisions.

For sex to be enjoyable and safe, what are the rules to abide by?

1. Ensure there's consent. If there's no consent and you act on it, it is rape. If the person is too intoxicated to provide consent, it is rape. If the person is too young to provide consent, it is rape. If the person is physically old enough but psychologically young to provide consent, it is rape. Consent happens when two individuals mutually agree to have sex in the right state of mind.

2. Be safe. Educate yourself about STDs and Pregnancies. Sex becomes unenjoyable when you begin to worry about both. Use a condom or appropriate form of birth control to avoid both so you can enjoy without having to worry.

3. Be spontaneous. Spontaneity creates excitement. Most individuals generally wait until they get into a bedroom to have sex. Eventually, sex becomes monotonous and less exciting. The best way to make sex enjoyable is to be spontaneous. If you feel the need to have sex in the bathroom, do so. If you feel the urge in the kitchen, have sex in the kitchen. If you are driving and can safely pull over to a private— non-offensive—location, have sex in the car.

4. Utilize other enjoyable methods. There is a variety of ways to enjoy sex with your partner. You can use toys, engage in role plays, and find exotic vacation spots. Whatever you do, always make sure you have fun, there's consent, and you're safe.

Mental Health Savage Challenge

Plan a sex date with your partner. Make it special. Have fun

Set effective boundaries

#BuildingBoundaries

B oundaries! Boundaries! Boundaries! In history, countries have created borders to control the flow of people in either direction. The same goes for all relationships we have in our lives. Have you taught people how to treat you? Have you told your friends, family, and coworkers about your likes and dislikes? A majority of people will say "No" to this! Guaranteed! Why? Because we expect others to figure it out as we go. The problem with that tactic is, you are likely to experience emotional discomfort before that happens.

For instance, if you like your toothpaste placed in a toothpaste holder and your new significant other doesn't know this, it might be left on the sink. It might get you upset, and you may not react immediately till about the third time it happens. How's it fair to be upset with your significant other when this wasn't communicated upfront?

Boundaries!

When I was younger, I realized that I hated people touching my food. It made me physically and psychologically uncomfortable. However, I was too conscious about this and didn't say anything until the touching became frequent. One day, I was at a dinner date with a new girl I had just met.

Trying to be romantic, she reached out to pick a piece of boneless chicken from my plate and tried to place it in my mouth. I saw it in slow motion. It felt like my soul was about to jump out of my skin, and she could tell I was upset. For the first time, I informed her that I don't like people touching my food. She smiled and said, okay. Ever since then, I decided to tell everyone I meet in a family gathering, office setting, or with friends, "Please don't touch my food. If you do, do it when I am not looking." It has become a joke around my social circle, but for now, no one does.

The moral of the story is everyone has boundaries that should not be crossed. How do you set boundaries?

You can do so assertively.

- Explain what you like and what you don't like ahead of time.
- Don't ignore inappropriate behaviors towards you. It doesn't matter who it is, if they are paying your bills, or if you owe them a lot of money. You have a fundamental human right to be treated with decency, or people will continue to treat you the way you allow them too.
- Respect other people's boundaries also. This is the golden rule. Treat people the way you want to be treated. If you don't want your friends just showing up at your house randomly, don't randomly show up at theirs either.
- Don't be afraid to walk away from someone who isn't respecting your boundaries. If you don't, they'll continue to break the boundaries.

Mental Health Savage Challenge

Create a boundary with someone challenging in your life using the above tips. Do so, assertively.

Avoid people pleasing

I call people-pleasing a disease because it puts the body at dis-ease. People-pleasing is defined as doing more for others than you do for yourself, prioritizing helping others at the expense of yourself, or emptying your water bottle for others, before working on re-filling it for yourself.

Religious texts have talked about loving others and loving one's self. The love you have for yourself will determine how much you can give to others before burning out. So, what's people-pleasing?

- People-pleasing is being in a relationship with someone that is not willing to give back.
- People-pleasing is trying to help someone who isn't trying to help themselves.
- People-pleasing is tolerating emotional, psychological, or physical pain because you fear being alone.
- People-pleasing is avoiding a favorable situation or person because a negative person doesn't get along with it.
- People-pleasing is not being able to assert your needs.
- People-pleasing is being afraid to say NO.

Get the picture?

In psychology, there's a term called cognitive dissonance. Cognitive dissonance occurs when your thoughts and actions don't match.

For instance, Rachel's best friend asks for a ride to work. Rachel's work schedule and home responsibilities make it almost impossible for her to provide the ride without jeopardizing both responsibilities. Rachel says yes to the ride for two months straight. Meanwhile, her best friend has several options that could be less stressful. This has affected Rachel's work performance.

Now, there's nothing wrong with providing a ride for your best friend. However, think of relationships as a two-way street. If Rachel's best friend has other options, a simple encouragement to use other options may pose less stress.

People usually have three responses to people-pleasing situations.

1. They may have a passive response or perform a task because they're too afraid or cannot say NO.
2. They may have an aggressive response. An aggressive response usually comes after tons of passive responses.
3. They may have an assertive response. An assertive response requires compromise. For instance, in Rachel's case. Rachel could say, "I can't do it every day of the week because of my job, but I can do two out of the five days, and I can teach you how to utilize uber or our other friends."

Remember, avoiding people pleasing doesn't mean that you need to reject every offer for help, but prioritize your convenience first so that you can help with the fullness of your heart and resources.

One more example.

James wants a promotion at work. So, every single time

another colleague calls off, he volunteers to take overtime. At first, it wasn't a problem, but eventually, he began to burn out. Unfortunately, because his boss knows James has formed that habit, James is the first person he asks for overtime opportunities. James always reluctantly says yes to it because he doesn't want to disappoint his boss.

He could be assertive and take one overtime opportunity out of every three requests. If he continues to be passive, he will eventually have an aggressive response to it due to his stress.

Don't People please for the sake of your mental health.

Mental Health Savage Challenge

Figure out the people in your life who directly or indirectly force you to people-please. Please, talk to your Therapist or friend about a way to avoid these behaviors.

Participate in a Volunteer activity

Human beings are built for connection, and one of the best connections you can make is when you are doing something for free, out of the goodness of your heart. The world needs volunteers for crisis nurseries, disaster reliefs, food banks, religious events, domestic violence shelters, kids summer camps. Etc.

Research shows that humans helping humans is a natural high. There is a release of dopamine and oxytocin when we volunteer to do activities for others.

Alcoholics Anonymous, Narcotics Anonymous, Cocaine Anonymous, and all other twelve step meetings rely on volunteers to help others. The idea of sponsorship is not just about helping a fellow addict. It is about indirectly helping one's self.

There's an innate universal reward for volunteering your time. Money is easy to give, but your time, that's something entirely different.

Remember, volunteering doesn't necessarily mean you have to spend hours of your day at a local shelter. Volunteering could be as simple as providing free advice to someone in need. Volunteering could be setting up a group chat for friends who need emotional support. You can volunteer by cooking a meal for a neighbor; you know struggles with having food.

Volunteering is anything that takes you outside of yourself, your work, your school, etc. Volunteering is loving and connecting.

Mental Health Savage Challenge

Take a picture of yourself doing a volunteer activity. Use hashtag #PeoplehelpingPeople

Pass your knowledge of mental health to your kids

One of the most significant issues I have with society today is how society talks about mental health. Lol actually, no one truly talks about mental health until they are struggling with mental illness.

Schools are overly focused on finding X and Y's value in algebra and do not teach kids true life skills and true coping skills. Everyone gets sad. Everyone gets angry. Everyone gets frustrated and anxious. Yet, if I asked a kindergartener, middle schooler, and high schooler to name five coping skills for each issue, they can't tell me.

Interestingly, parents who have also gone through mental health stressors don't know either. Part of mental health advocacy is to pass down knowledge. If you are struggling with depression, for instance, chances are your kids may go through it at some point in their life. The majority of mental illnesses are genetic. Life happens regardless of whether we want or don't want it.

Kids need to know. Teaching a kid that grounding technique helps with anxiety saves them from growing up feeling helpless about anxiety attacks. If you can teach a kid about what it means to be depressed, have mood swings, etc., they will grow up not feeling alone.

Many teenagers I work with have reported feeling ashamed to tell anyone that they cut, have suicidal thoughts, are depressed, can't control their moods, etc. Many of them have reported feeling "weird" because they have panic attacks.

Society isn't effectively teaching kids that many people have mental health struggles, and it is okay not to be okay.

A teenage boy I knew struggled with social anxiety. He didn't know why. All he knew was that he hated being in school. The teacher labeled him as truant because he would skip classes. He was suspended for skipping classes (I know the logic doesn't make any sense). If the school focused on his mental health, they would have recognized that he struggled with social anxiety. Because he thought he was weird, he later found out about alcohol and soon began attending classes again, but with a bottle of vodka that looked like water. He began drinking every day and soon became addicted to alcohol at a young age. All this could have been prevented if he had adequate knowledge about his struggles with social anxiety.

In counseling, he was able to work on his social anxiety by challenging himself to be around a group of people that he was uncomfortable with. Eventually, he realized that he didn't need a vodka shot to have a conversation with a stranger. Finally, he realized that approaching girls wasn't as difficult as he thought.

Again, mental health advocacy goes beyond letting older people know that mental illness exists. Suppose we can focus on a bottom-up perspective. In that case, we can target feelings of inadequacy present in the young population, so when mental health stressors come up, they can identify and deal with it in a healthy way.

Remember, it's all about healthy coping skills because there are many unhealthy coping skills.

Another example is of a young woman I worked with. Let's call her Jane. Jane is a 15-year-old with symptoms of depression that has been ongoing for two years. Her parents didn't know for a while. She was treated for depression for years before everyone realized that her diagnosis wasn't depression. She had a bipolar diagnosis. Mother is diagnosed with Bipolar II Disorder, and her grandmother is Bipolar. Yet both never taught her what to expect and how to handle it.

Teaching kids about what you have struggled with is teaching them how to handle it. It is teaching them to de-stigmatize it as well.

I am looking forward to a day where mental exercises are added to the school curriculum the same way physical exercises are prioritized. It is not just about educating kids about how to deal with mental stressors. It is about teaching kids how to recognize it in themselves and others. It is about learning general coping skills, treatment options, and live examples.

Mental Health Savage Challenge

If you are struggling with mental illness or have knowledge about mental illnesses, tell your kids, nieces, or other loved ones. Knowledge is power.

Chapter 6

Introspect

#ConciousRelaxation

Meditation is the gym for the mind

The very first time I heard about meditation was in graduate school. It was not something I paid attention to in high school or during my undergraduate career. I did not understand why anyone would want to be quiet and focus within. However, I remember the play dates I used to have as a child. My friend's mother used to make us have one hour of "quiet time" daily. I dreaded going to visit my friend just because of that.

I mean, why would you ask a 5-year-old to be quiet for one hour, after lunchtime? That was when we had the most energy. We had to turn off all electronics. We were not allowed to talk, play, or move from our designated seating areas. It was like a daily time-out punishment. The only thing we were allowed to do was read. It didn't have to be schoolwork. We were allowed to read a book, the bible, or just sit and reflect. It used to be the longest hour of my day.

Fast forward back to my adult life, I now appreciate those moments because I didn't realize how loud the world was. For instance, on a given day, we look at our phones more than fifty times. If we are not getting a text, we are getting a tweet, Facebook message, Snapchat Message, or an Instagram notification. Every year, more phone apps are created to take a chunk of our attention.

Interestingly, that is just our phone. Our phones are a small chunk of our life. There are also media, billboards, news stations, radio stations, car sticker ads, restaurant ads, etc. We are constantly bombarded with;

"Hey, look at me!"

"I'm right here!"

"You need to buy this!"

"This will make your life better."

"This is what is going on in the world that you need to know,"

"Hello! We can help you!"

And then you wonder why you are stressed all day. Even if we are not paying attention to each ad, news, or media, our brain is. Our mind is gathering all this information and sifting through important and unimportant ones. All of these are happening unconsciously. Inevitably, we are putting undue pressure on our brains.

Then there is another chunk of stress that is added to our lives. We go to work, school, take care of kids, take care of other family members, cook, clean, drive to pick up groceries— we are always on the move. After all of this, we choose to watch a television show or movie. Unknowing to us, television programs and films are bombarded with advertisements of liquor, wine, clothes, shoes, houses, and lifestyle.

Now, my question is, what time do you get to shut it all off?

Your brain needs "Conscious rest."

That is what meditation is. What will it be like if you can shut it all off? Turn off the television, phone, and all technology. Find a place to sit, close your eyes, and tune off all external noise so you can focus within.

When you meditate, you don't have to cross your leg, place your palms on your knees, and *hum.* You can keep it simple. Because of today's society's fast-paced nature, I recommend doing this either before bed or right when you wake up.

1. Get comfortable
2. Turn on a guided meditation. You can find these in the app stores, YouTube or music streaming services.
3. You can turn on relaxing music. I find classical music to be the most helpful.
4. Breathe in through your nose and out through your mouth. Deep breaths allow the intake of positive energy and the expulsion of negative energy. It also helps reduce the heart rate and increase blood flow.
5. Try not to focus on the past or future. Bring your awareness to how your body and mind feels right now.
6. If you find your mind drifting towards the past or the future, it is okay. Just try to return to the present. Remember that meditation isn't the absence of thought; it is the awareness of it.
7. You can have fun with meditation. Picture yourself in your favorite place; the beach, childhood bedroom, playground, mall, ocean, etc. Then walk around this place in your mind. The mind is extremely powerful. Research shows that sometimes, the mind cannot tell the difference between what is happening and what you are thinking about.

An experiment done with athletes proved this. They were asked to run a race in their mind. Interestingly, the same muscles that would be fired if they actually ran were fired by just thinking about it.

Some of the benefits of meditation include reduced stress, anxiety, and depression. Meditation has also been shown to improve memory, regulate mood, and induce serenity.

***Mental Health Savage Challenge ***

Show us how you meditate using the hashtag #ConsciousRelaxation

The power of Mindfulness

#Mindfulness

The first time I heard of mindfulness, I cringed. Where I am from, "be mindful" is a threat. It is like saying, "watch what you are doing" or "be careful." "Be mindful" was something said to help the other person reflect on consequences.

For mental health, mindfulness means remaining aware of the present. That's it. The past doesn't matter because it already happened. The future? You don't even know what I will say in the next paragraph, so why are you stressing about it? Pay attention to now. Pay attention to the words. Pay attention to the voice you hear in your head as you read this. Is it the sound of my voice, or is it the sound of your voice? What does your room smell like? What can you hear in the background? The fan? The tv? Everything that is going on right now is like a symphony. It is music for those who are willing to experience it.

Stop reading right now. Look at the pages of this book or the device you are reading from; how does it feel? What does it smell like? What does it look like? Is it heavy?

When I was seventeen years old, my father bought Bose headphones for me. Looking back now, I wish I had never used those headphones. Ever since then, the quality of music

I hear doesn't sound the same on most platforms. I went to the gas station to buy cheap earphones. I was disappointed. For most cars I buy, the quality of the speakers matters to me.

If you practice mindfulness regularly, you will begin to see and feel a shift in your consciousness. This shift in consciousness will make it difficult to imagine what life was like without mindfulness.

When you're driving on the highway, pay attention to the landscape. Watch how the landscapes emerge as you are moving forward. Watch the trees, buildings, and see how beautiful life is.

When you have ice cream, don't just lick it, feel it. Feel the layers of cream dissolving into your throat. Feel how it transports itself from your tongue to your throat then down to your stomach. For real, I am serious, try it. It is blissful. It feels so great. But here is the thing, once you try it, it will feel strange to go through an ice cream cone in seconds, mindlessly.

When was the last time you woke up early to watch the sunrise?

When was the last time you watched the sunset?

Nature has given us so much to admire, and yet we choose four walls and television. Our bodies are not designed to be indoors. Our bodies are designed to appreciate nature's creation. Our bodies are designed to be around nature, species, and plants.

So how do you practice mindfulness?

It is simple. You can practice mindfulness doing anything.

Like pizza? Have a friend order a random pizza, sit down in a calm, quiet place, without looking at what's in the box.

Close your eyes, breathe, pull out a slice of pizza, and eat slowly. Guess the sauce and the toppings used. Chances are, if you eat it too fast, you won't know. But if you eat it slowly and let the spices, sauce, cheese, chicken…pineapples—lol. Yes, I said pineapples—don't just taste it, feel the ingredients.

You can practice mindfulness in the shower. Start with a hot shower and slowly reduce the temperature until it is cold. Feel the water on your skin. Don't rush! Just feel it. It's amazing.

You can practice mindfulness in traffic. Put on your favorite song. Crank the volume up. Not too loud. Find that perfect medium where you can still hear all the instruments without that overly prioritized bass. Try to guess the musical instruments used. Listen to the drums, flute, trumpet, tempo of the sounds, everything. Take it in.

You can practice mindfulness with your sense of smell. Some people like the smell of oranges while others like rain. Everyone likes a unique scent. It is usually tied to a pleasant memory. Find out what you want and find the scent for it. Bath and Bodyworks has a collection of scented candles that I find pretty impressive. It is almost always close to the real thing. You can also take it upon yourself to smell something that is actually in front of you—like an orange, a brand-new book, or a brand-new car.

Mindfulness may seem like a chore at first, but eventually, it will become muscle memory if you keep practicing it.

If you are not mindful, you could travel from where you are to another city and not remember anything in between. If you are not mindful, you could eat your whole meal and not truly taste it. If you are not mindful, you will hear an entire song and not listen to it. If you are not mindful, you can live with your significant other for years and not truly explain why you find them beautiful.

Mindfulness has been proven to help depression and

anxiety. This is because you are focused on the sensations of what is happening now. Not what has happened or what will happen. It will help you become more self-aware. Self-awareness allows you to become conscious of your emotional triggers. If you become self-aware, you'll drift towards self-mastery. You will begin to learn what you like and why you like it. Be mindful.

Mental Health Savage Challenge

Share how you practice mindfulness using #Mindfulness

Buy a Journal

#DailyJournal

The very first time I saw someone journal was on the television show, Vampire Diaries. I was amazed because I understood that journaling is all about history. Stefan, the main character, has been a vampire for over 100 years and has journaled every day since. Looking back, I wish I had immediately begun the habit of journaling, but I didn't. Four years after that day, I started journaling daily.

Journaling helped with self-reflection. It helped me identify what went wrong that day, what went well, and what could be improved. It helped me with gratitude. For instance, if I had a bad day on Monday, June 20th, I can look back at the emotional state I was in and realize that I made it to July 30th in one piece despite the catastrophic events that occurred.

Okay, that being said, let's address some of the stereotypes of journaling;

1. Journaling does not have to begin with "Dear Diary." You are not talking to the book you are writing in; you are reflecting in-wards to yourself.
2. Journaling does not have to be done in the bedroom. You can journal anywhere; living room, bedroom, at work, at school, on the bus, while waiting for your

meal, wherever you feel comfortable. If you have a bag, take it with you.

3. Journaling does not have to be done in a physical book. It can be done on an app on your phone. You can log your journals on there. Having a physical copy stuck in one location (the bedroom) diminishes variety and ability to remember thoughts. For instance, if your goal is to be aware of times, you feel most anxious during the day, by journaling your thoughts. Chances are, you are not going to remember at night when you are in bed.

4. Journaling does not have to be done daily. It can be done hourly, weekly, or even monthly. The pressure most people feel to journal may cause them to forget about journaling. Again, the goal is to do something you are most comfortable with. Set a goal for yourself if you struggle with journaling. Start monthly, then bi-monthly, then bi-weekly, then every other day. You become a pro when you can do it daily, consistently, for 60 days. At that point, you have built a habit.

5. Your journal does not have to be in a private area. When I ask most people why they don't journal, they say it is because they don't want others to see it. If it makes you feel uncomfortable, find a journal that can be locked, or one with codes in it. However, if you don't care who sees it, leave it out in the open.

6. Journaling does not necessarily have to describe what happened throughout the day. Your journal can include poems, motivational quotes you're reflecting on, scriptures you reflect on, or even random words that come to your mind throughout the day. For instance, *why do crickets make a weird sound at night?*

7. Journals don't have to be written. You can make a video journal.

The bottom line is, make your journaling work for you because it can help reduce anxiety, help you understand

Tami Odimayo

patterns of behaviors that are beneficial or detrimental to you, and give you a space to vent.

Mental Health savage challenge

Challenge yourself to journal three times this week. #SavageJournal

Embrace Nature

#MyNaturalPeace

As said in the previous chapter, we are nature; therefore, we should take it upon ourselves to be around nature every day. We are nature; consequently, we should take it upon ourselves to avoid artificial ways of life. We are nature; therefore, we should be nature.

For example, in diet, if you are eating natural foods, in its natural state, in its natural portion, you are less likely to have to work extra hard to maintain your weight.

If you are taking time to implement natural physical activities, like walking, running, or even bike riding, you are less likely to need the gym.

If you are spending time meditating and practicing mindfulness with nature, you are less likely to experience anxiety.

Your body loves natural things and experiences because it doesn't have to evolve or adjust to whatever artificial element you are utilizing.

One of the most important advice I give is to watch animals. I have a dog who is on a strict routine. He wakes up around the time I wake up—at 6:30 am. He eats. He uses the bathroom. He plays around for a couple of hours, and when he is tired, he takes a nap.

I applied the same principles by trusting the natural instincts nature has given me. This can be done by using the five core areas of mental health.

1. Maintain a regular sleep schedule. No matter how redundant this may seem to you, sleep is one way our body naturally heals. During sleep, cells and muscle tissues are repaired. Your brain can relax. Practice good sleep hygiene by doing the following:
    a. Set a consistent sleep schedule.
    b. Try to eat at least three hours before bed.
    c. Your bedroom is for sleep and sex. Anything else will confuse your brain's associations with the bed and the bedroom.
    d. Limit the use of artificial lights during bedtime, e.g., phones, televisions, and lamps.
    e. Create a consistent bedtime routine so that your body is aware of when to sleep. For instance, if you like to drink tea before bedtime, be consistent with it.
    f. When you wake up in the middle of the night, avoid going to the fridge to snack. It is disrupting your body's rhythm and making you more likely to develop a bad habit.
    g. If insomnia persists, try a natural alternative like sleepy time chamomile tea.
    h. There's usually a time your body wakes up naturally, without an alarm. If you wake up before your alarm, get up and start your day because if you go back to sleep, you might be groggier when the alarm finally goes off.
2. Eat as natural as you can. I am not saying you should avoid the necessary fun of life. Lord knows ice cream is beneficial sometimes. Ice cream every day? Not a good idea for both mental and physical health.
3. Exercise thoroughly, even when outside of the gym.

If you can carry six grocery bags, do so instead of pushing a cart. If you can take the stairs, do so instead of using the elevator. Try your best to maintain natural activity.

4. Socialize. We are naturally social beings. We love to socialize with people, places, animals, and even things. We need connection and interaction. For example, my dog is sometimes all over me, and other times, he goes to a corner and relaxes. Every day, he gets his social needs met. It is important that we get our social needs met even outside of work.

5. Stress. Stress can be avoided if we focus on the other core areas of mental health.

Nature has given us every single thing that we need to survive and thrive. We just have to find it. Take some time with nature.

Drink water instead of soda.

Take a walk to the nearest grocery store instead of driving.

Open the windows to air out your homes instead of inhaling air conditioning air all day.

Find a clean lake to swim in, instead of a pool.

Go hiking.

Take your dog for a walk in a place that doesn't require a leash.

Instead of watching documentaries, take some time to experience bird watching.

Whatever your needs are, chances are, nature already has it.

Mental Health Savage Challenge**

Where do you find natural peace? Use hashtag #MyNaturalPeace

Create 30 minutes of self-reflection, daily

#SelfReflection

As humans, we are always on the go. We wake up, eat, go to work, school, eat some more, etc. you get the picture. The only time we have for self-reflection is usually the time before bed. Every other free time that we have is spent catching up with a Netflix tv show, social media account, or even an old friend.

Life happens, and life happens fast. Sometimes, it is highly beneficial to slow it down, and other times, it is helpful to speed it up. But slowing or speeding things up will not be beneficial without moments of reflection.

When I was younger, I noticed that my parents' punishments began to shift. They went from taking things away from me to giving me time outs or grounding me. These moments were not to be used to read a novel or engage in another distracting activity. My parents required me to write a self-reflection essay to reflect on whatever I had done wrong or right. I hated every moment of it. I mean, who wants to think about every grumpy statement and backtalk you have said to your parents, all day?

In my adult life, I realized that life happens at its own

pace. If you can take the time to reflect on your day, you can think about the conversations that could have gone better, you can think about how many steps you have taken towards achieving your goal, you can think about opportunities for growth that you may have missed.

You can engage in self-reflection by journaling, talking to a trusted companion, or meditating. One of the most powerful tools a human can ever have is the understanding of one's self. Self-awareness promotes a different kind of experience.

If you can understand why you are, you can understand what to be.

If you can understand who you are, you can understand your purpose and how to get there.

There are a lot of missed opportunities we experience daily. You could be seeking a relationship, and there's someone out there in front of you. However, due to the hecticness of life, you are unable to read the love signals the person has been sending to you. You might have missed an opportunity to ask for a raise but will never know because you are not reflecting on your day.

Remember, self-reflection doesn't mean you should hang on to the past. It simply means you should analyze and learn from it.

Mental Health Savage challenge

How do you self-reflect? Through poetry, stories, music, etc Share using Hashtag #SelfReflection

Take a vacation at least once every three months

You can go to your boss and say, "I read this one book, and it recommended I go on vacation regularly." You have worked hard at work, school, and at home. Everyone needs rest. However, rest doesn't necessarily imply sleeping all day. It doesn't mean going to Cancun or Jamaica and spending thousands of dollars. It simply means take an intentional day off for yourself and do something for yourself.

One of the best things to do for yourself is to go on vacation. Most individuals spend most of their "awake time" at work, at school, helping others, or all the above. That gives you about an hour to 3 hours of personal time for yourself before you go to bed. So out of 24 hours, you spend 9 hours going to, staying, and coming from work. If you are in school, you are dedicating anywhere from 2 hours to 5 hours for schoolwork. If you have kids or a family to take care of, that's another huge chunk of your day taken, and you haven't even considered sleep.

Vacation gives you time away from daily life stressors, allowing you to relax and evaluate the goals you have accomplished and the goals you are working on. As I said, a vacation doesn't have to be expensive. It doesn't even have to take multiple elongated days.

It could be driving to a different city and spoiling yourself with a new restaurant you haven't tried before. It could be a weekend at a hotel/motel with your spouse. It could even be going to an amusement/water park. Whatever it is, make sure it is enjoyable, relaxing, and something that takes your mind away from your stressors.

Mental Health Savage Challenge

Go on a vacation. Take a picture using #VacationisLife

Engage in cleaning environmental space

Not only is cleanliness effective for your physical health, it is useful for your mental health also. A sink full of dishes with decaying food will cause insects' infestations and expose you to horrible smells. Inhaling dust from your furniture directly affects your lungs. A clutter of disorganized objects could cause accidents. Research also shows that clutter makes it difficult to concentrate on tasks.

One common characteristic of severely depressive clients is a lack of motivation to do anything, especially clean— your environmental space matters. Let us imagine that every item in your household is energy. The chair, the tables, the television, the dishes, the broom, the vacuum cleaner, the lamp etc…it is all energy. Now, picture this. Imagine water flowing through your environment. Is it going to flow naturally, or will it have places where it gets stuck?

I watched a minimalist documentary. It gave me a concept of cleanliness that I never thought of. Generally speaking, an anxious brain is a cluster of disorganized worries. What will happen if one can organize those worries?

I have personally found that organizing my household and office helps with my mental health. Here's how I do it.

1. I realized that we are in a generation of acquiring "stuff." In this book, stuff is something you can do without. Do you really need a brand-new outfit for that one event? How many shoes is enough? Realizing this, I created a system. Every six months, I engage in a de-clutter process. Anything in my household that I haven't used in six months to a year, I either sell it or give it away to someone who needs it more. Try it. Not only are you blessing others with a gift, but you are also making room for what matters.

2. Meditate while vacuuming the house. I realized that chores seem overbearing. I mean, our parents indirectly made us hate chores by treating chores like a punishment. Change the dynamic of what chores feel like to you and make it fun. Turn on some music, inspirational YouTube video, podcast, or meditation exercise. Listen while cleaning. It helps relieve stress.

3. Separate needs from wants. Needs are essential. Wants are semi-essential. You can save money, time, and space by understanding this principle.

4. It doesn't have to be perfect for it to be clean. A majority of people want to clean everything at once and then wonder why cleaning is draining. Select a day to vacuum, select another day to dust. Select a day to clean the bathroom, choose another day to clean the rust. Don't overwhelm yourself with cleaning tasks, or it will not be enjoyable.

5. Remember that your physical health and mental health work together.

Mental Health Savage Challenge

Show us a before and after picture of a space you just cleaned using the hashtag #Cluttercleanseday

Chapter 7

Advocacy

#MentalHealthSavage

How to be a Mental Health Savage

I am looking forward to a day where people go for yearly Mental Health checkups, the same way they go for physical checkups. I am looking forward to a day where employers add paid mental health days to their benefit lists. I am looking forward to a day where schools have Mental Health Education classes like PE classes.

I am looking forward to a day where things don't have to be extremely bad for people to seek mental health counseling services.

Mental Health is everything. It determines how we navigate life. It affects our relationships with others, affects our ability to learn, affects our ability to function at our employment, and affects how we perceive ourselves. So, why is society still not at this level of awareness?

This chapter is about advocacy, personal advocacy, relational advocacy, educational advocacy, and political advocacy.

How can you begin this process?

1. If you feel your mental health is important, begin to practice what you preach. People around you will learn by example. When you prioritize your mental health, you begin to glow differently. That glow is what people will see. What people see going well for you is what they will start doing. `GlowByExample`

2. If you have kids, start teaching them about the importance of understanding and recognizing their emotions. The earlier kids start, the easier it is for them in adulthood. Often, I have seen that individuals don't even understand exactly what they are feeling. That's why they either feel extreme anxiety or numbness. If your four-year-old is crying, simply ask, "How do you feel?" Because crying doesn't necessarily mean sadness. People cry when they are frustrated, happy, angry, afraid, or even surprised. `#PreachToTheKids`

3. Advocate for mental health at your job. Talk about meditation, mindfulness, deep breathing, etc. When employees effectively work on their mental health, they will be more productive. `#MentalHealthAdvocacy`

4. Legislative efforts can be made on a local, state, and even national level. Little drops of water make a mighty ocean. If 200 people read this book, 200 people are actively teaching others about mental health. `#MHPolitics`

5. Remind yourself and others that there's nothing to be ashamed of. Society has created a stigma for something typical. Celebrities, scholars of history, politicians, pastors, philosophers—have all struggled with their mental health at some point. If you are in a position of power, say something. `#VIPmentalhealth`

Mental Health Savage Challenge

Tami Odimayo

Demonstrate mental health advocacy during mental health awareness month or any other time of the year. Make or share a post related to your mental health or statistics of any mental illness that is more prevalent in your close circle of friends or family. Use hashtag #MentalHealthSavage

Chapter 8
The BLT Approach
#BLTapproach

Identify and execute your purpose

My motto is to be yourself, live with intention, and trust your instincts. Every human is born with a purpose. Every human is born with a gift. Every human is born with a talent. The problem we have with today's world is that most people don't know their purpose. A majority of people are living the dreams that others have designed for them. A majority of people are seeking and living in what's ideal versus what is real to them.

Your purpose in life is what gets you up in the morning, excited. Your purpose is what makes you feel happy.

If you are not doing what the universe has designed you to do, if you are not in a relationship the universe has intended for you, if you are not in the job the universe has intended for you, you will feel discomfort. That discomfort will be expressed as depression, anxiety, insomnia, etc. Spend life seeking and walking towards your purpose, and you will experience bliss.

Before I go into the "how," I'll give you an example

I know a psychologist who spent years providing counseling to others and then decided to quit his job to become a bicycle repairman. He has found more fulfillment in repairing the bicycles of others than counseling.

There is a Medical Doctor who quit his medical career, making more than four hundred thousand dollars a year, who became a Pilot, earning less than half of that.

I have met a master's degree holder who is experiencing more bliss being a janitor than having a desk job.

ur happiness has nothing to do with your career or how much you are making. Your happiness has to do with what you are doing to seek your purpose.

So how do you find your purpose?

BE YOURSELF

Take off your mask. Your environment is continuously shaping your character and personality. We watch movies and television shows, and we sometimes imitate characters we see and people we see in real life. These imitations are unconscious. The problem is, a lot of people cannot tell the difference between their mask and their true selves. Unfortunately, the mask you are wearing attracts people attracted to the mask, not you. Invariably, you attract the wrong people and situations into your life.

For instance, if you want bigger breasts, and you get breast surgery. The people you will attract are people that like bigger breasts. If you like women who read because you like to read, going to a club to find a woman isn't a good idea because she would most likely like partiers.

Being yourself means being true to your emotions. There are things that you like to do naturally. If you like to swim in the ocean, don't live in a desert. If you like the sun, don't live in Alaska. If you enjoy cleaning, clean. If you like to write, write. If you like to speak and motivate, be a motivational speaker. If you like to act, be an actor or actress. If you like to heal, become the type of healer you prefer. Whatever it is, be it.

There's a natural joy from doing the things you love and being yourself. Some individuals might say, "but what if I cannot be those things, fully?"

My response is you don't have to do everything on a large scale, but take a step towards it. If you are a healer and know you cannot become a Medical Doctor, there are other forms of healers. If you like to swim in the ocean and can only afford to live by a lake, do so. If you enjoy acting and cannot go to Hollywood to fulfill your dreams, start a drama club in your area, and organize plays. If you like to write, you don't have to be a New York Times bestseller to become a writer. Start a blog. As long as you are doing what you love, your body will reward you with happiness.

Once you understand your passions, the next step is to set goals towards that passion. This is where the next point comes into play.

LIVE WITH INTENTION

Living with intention means living your life based on your goals. Your goals don't have to be big, but you have to have a goal—something that wakes you up in the morning. If you like bike riding, set a goal to ride an additional mile every day. Let your life be evolved around your purpose.

For instance, Jacob wants to become a politician. He recently began his election campaign to become a city councilman. For him, living with intention will mean abstaining from anyone or anything that may taint his electoral image.

Every day you wake up, with everything you do, and every person you meet, ask yourself, "Is this going to take me away from my goal or towards my goal?"

If it is going to take you away from your goals, don't do it. If it is going to take you towards your goal, do it. Take a step towards the building of your talent. If you like to dance, take some dance lessons or watch YouTube videos and practice in your bedroom.

If you do this, happiness is guaranteed, and stress will be reduced.

The body loves it when you are doing what it was built for.

Living with intention in regards to your physical and mental health also means doing the things that benefit all core areas of your health.

TRUST YOUR INSTINCTS

Your body will tell you when something is not right. Listen to your instincts. Cultivate it. Often, we feel anxious in particular situations because we need to do something to change it. A lot of times, we feel depressed because we need to do something to change our situation. The body rebels when you are not doing what it wants, so learn to listen to it.

In counseling, a primary focus is to recognize your triggers. Triggers are what puts you in a state of discomfort. You become aware of your triggers when you become mindful. Mindfulness allows you to trust your instincts. That friend that gives you an off vibe is probably doing something that's not right.

We are beings of energy, and energy communicates with us.

I am sure everyone reading this has walked into a room of people and felt a tense vibe even when they are pretending to be happy. Trust those vibes. It never lies.

If you are doing something you love, you will feel good about it. You will feel joy. If you are doing something that will negatively affect your purpose, you won't feel good about it.

Tami Odimayo

Suppose you are struggling with mental illness and seeing a therapist, psychiatrist, or another healer, set small goals to make things better and move towards bigger goals. Remember, Rome wasn't built in a day. Be patient with yourself.

Mental Health Savage Challenge

How can you apply the BLT approach to your life? Share using the hashtag #BLTapproach

Practice the power of positive thinking

The first time I heard about the law of attraction, I laughed at it. I was like, "there is no way I can change my life by just adjusting my thoughts. All that is mystical nonsense." But then I sat and truly evaluated my life. Every time I struggled, my mental health struggled more because of my thoughts.

One day, I came across the movie, *the Secret*. If you have not seen it, you need to. It is one of the most powerful documentaries I have ever seen.

Anyways, when I saw it for the first time, I was in my parent's house, shortly after graduating with my bachelor's degree, with no job and no hope for a job. My mental health was in terrible shape, and as a result, my physical health was even worse. I immediately decided to create a vision board—a white sheet of paper that I had gotten from the university library.

I immediately wrote down a list of things that I wanted to accomplish in the next year and taped it to my wardrobe door so that anytime I was getting dressed, I could at least glance at it.

That exact day, I sent in three applications online. I

decided to get dressed. I wore a nice shirt, some slacks, and a blazer. I borrowed my mother's car and went to those jobs to follow up on an application I had just turned in less than two hours ago.

The first job I went to said they hadn't gotten my application. So, they offered me a paper application. While I was filling it out, my future boss walked out of the office, looked at me from head to toe, and told me to come in the very next day for an interview.

The second and third job told me I had to wait until the application I sent was processed. Long story short. I got the first job I walked into. The interview wasn't even an interview. I came in to sign my letter of employment and spent thirty minutes joking around.

Soon after, I realized this positive thinking thing was working. I decided to imagine myself in a car. I even bought a car air freshener at Walmart in anticipation of a car. Two weeks later, my father offered to go half on a car for me. It wasn't the best car, but I loved the heck out of the car. It had no A/C, but it was my mini future Mercedes.

I then decided to imagine what it would be like to have my apartment, a new car, a relationship, better physical health, a career, be an author, and the rest is history.

The mind is powerful. If you can think it, you can be it.

Positive thinking allows you to refocus your attention away from failures and focus on successes instead.

For instance, two brothers grew up in an intensely abusive home. Because of this, both brothers did everything in their power to avoid their home life. One brother joined a gang, and the other spent his free time in the library. When I sat with both brothers, one brother said, "I'm in a gang because my father is very abusive. He hits my mother every day. I hate him. I just hope he dies. He doesn't do anything. He just looks for a way to hurt us. I want nothing to do with him, and I hate my mother for staying with him."

The other brother said, "I realized that my father is an alcoholic. My mother struggles with depression and low self-esteem. I realize that hating both of them wouldn't do me any good. That's why I study hard enough to go to college and have the resources to help them."

Two brothers. Similar experiences. Two different perspectives.

Some people say, "well, the reality of the situation is that things are bad." No one is negating that. Things are bad, but for every bad situation, there is a good outlook.

Let me give you another example. Often, we dream about big dreams and forget that to achieve these dreams, there might be some loss. *There is a friend of mine who always loved computers. Unfortunately, he studied finance and didn't want to go back to school. While he was working at a bank, he taught himself how to code. Soon after, he lost his job and couldn't find any job for months. He was depressed but decided to continue to learn how to code. He finally found a job that had nothing to do with finance or computers. It paid less than his previous job but gave him more time to learn how to code. When there was an opportunity for a promotion, his boss always gave him an excuse and promoted someone else. This significantly increased his anxiety at the workplace. However, he decided to be positive and continued to learn how to code.*

One day, he had a conversation with someone about his work experience and his part-time hobby at a coffee shop. He got set up for an interview at a major credit card company, that paid him more than three times the amount of money he was earning at his current job. But that wasn't the blessing. The blessing was that he got to do his two passions at his new job; finance and computer coding. When he looks back, he realized that he would never have been at the coffee shop that night if he had gotten the promotion. If he didn't meet that person, he wouldn't have gotten the new job. Also, being fired from the bank gave him enough time to work on his computer coding project.

The difference between a depressed person and a non-depressed person is the ability to think positively. The difference between an anxious person and a non-anxious person is the ability to think positively. The difference between an addict and a recovering person is the ability to think positively. Everything revolves around thinking positively. Everything.

One last example; In my days working at an outpatient rehabilitation center. I met a chronically alcoholic client. Many people may not know this, but being addicted to alcohol feels like a death sentence because triggers are everywhere. Almost every grocery store, gas station, friend's house, and even restaurants have alcohol. Unlike cocaine, meth, and heroine, it is virtually impossible to avoid seeing alcohol daily. Even on television, there are tons of alcohol advertisements. You get the picture. Alcohol is difficult to quit.

When I met him, he was depressed. He had lost his wife, children, house, car, and business because of his alcoholism. People in his community knew him as "the drunk." In cases like these, my first goal is to focus on gratitude. What are you grateful for? I asked. He didn't know. But eventually said, "Life." My general belief is as long as there's life, there's hope. The universe can continue to move in your favor.

I recommended that the book the power of positive thinking. He read it, and the very next day, it was like I met a different man. He began to see that losing his wife wasn't as bad as he thought. He realized that despite all the money he had, he wasn't happy. So eventually, he stopped sulking about losing his house, car, and business. He wore a smile to all his sessions every day. He took every suggestion that he could get from outpatient counselors. Despite his legal issues, he chose to focus on the fact that he was still alive and well.

When he got his three-month sobriety date, he was allowed to start spending time with his children. Soon, his children spent more time with him than his ex-wife because he became a generally happy and bubbly individual. On his six-month sobriety date, he said to me, "I make a whole lot less money. I have no companion. I spend more time fixing my car than driving it, yet I am happy. If I didn't lose all the things I lost, I would not be in this building talking to you. I would not know that as long as I watch the thoughts that get into my head, I can be happy." It is his one-year anniversary date as of the publication of this book. The last time I spoke to him, he told me that his ex-wife, who called him a dead beat, now wants him back. Guess what he told her!? No! Why? "She is a negative person. She will affect my thoughts, and I will be back to where I used to be."

Your thoughts matter!

Your physical health, the friends you have, and the life you live can all be changed when you seek the positive aspects.

Mental Health Savage Challenge

Make a vision board. Where do you want to see yourself in a year? What do you want in two years, three years, four years, and even five years? What routine do you wish to establish daily? What are you most grateful for? Create a vision board. Take a picture of it and post using hashtag #PositiveThoughtsPositiveLife

Watch yourself grow.

Find a profession that matches your purpose

#BallingwithmyPurpose

M any individuals spend a considerable chunk of their lives at work and dedicate a small amount of time to personal growth. For instance, the average individual works eight hours a day—and that is the average. Most individuals have commitments after work, like childcare and other adult obligations. Let's just say you get off work at 5 pm, run some errands, eat, take care of kids, family, etc. If you go to bed at 10 pm, there's only a small chunk of time left for you to relax by yourself.

If you spend most of your day doing what you love, it won't feel like work.

That's why this rule is essential. In my counseling sessions, I sometimes slip a random question. The answer isn't important. I am looking for how long it takes to figure out the answer. I would usually ask;

"Why are you here?"

Most of the time, I get a confused look. And sometimes, the response goes, "I need to work on my mental health, trauma, marriage, relationship, resentments, etc."

Then I rephrase the question;

"Why are you on earth? What is your purpose? What is your meaning in life?"

Sometimes, the response I get discourages me from going further. For instance, a client has responded by saying, "What does this have to do with anything?" Other times, there is a long pause that could last up to five minutes.

"I never really thought about that."

Or

"That's a tough one."

As an Existential Therapist, my job is to help my clients navigate towards identifying their purpose. I believe that if an individual does not identify their purpose and work towards their purpose, the individual will continue to experience a constant state of dissatisfaction.

This is how I phrase it. "If you are not doing what your body and the universe designed you to do, you're bound to feel depressed and anxious,"

This may be a bold statement, but its fruits are highly beneficial. For example, there was a gentleman in the banking industry I had worked with. He made a significant amount of money. He had a wife, kids, and a beautiful home. He was able to enjoy lush vacations. Despite this, he still faced significant symptoms of depression. I started to explore his interest and discovered his love for art. He was a talented artist. I challenged him to set time aside to work on art. As the weeks passed by, I could visibly see his excitement blossoming. The more he painted, the better he felt.

His body rewarded him by increasing his dopamine each time he did what he loved.

Tami Odimayo

I challenged another client of mine to take it a step further. He is a construction worker who loves poetry. At first, I didn't think he was a good poet. He wrote down a couple of poems right in front of me, and I was awed. I challenged him to set up a website, social media account, or join a live spoken word poetry event. After a few weeks, he was able to channel his cravings for illicit substances into his poetry. Whenever he craved drugs, he would write.

I had another client who had a high paying state job. His job responsibilities had nothing to do with his natural interest. He loved philosophy and highly intellectual activities. He didn't like getting out of bed, hated his job, isolated himself from his family, and used drugs to compensate for these feelings. Each time I met with him, I challenged him with a philosophical idea. We spent the first twenty minutes of our session discussing this philosophical idea. Each time, I noticed how he would light up. Even though his reason for coming to see a Therapist had nothing to do with identifying his purpose, I noticed that focusing on this brought him natural joy.

k your natural gift, find your purpose, and use that as a driving mechanism to help others.

There are tons of people going to jobs they don't like because it pays better. These people will stay in these jobs till they retire. Imagine what your life will be like if you are doing what you love. Imagine what your life will be like if you learned ways to grow your natural gifts. Imagine finding a way to make a living out of your natural gift. Every talent is useful to this world. Every gift is valuable. If you're studying in a program you love, it will feel enjoyable. If you're working for a job you're passionate about, it won't feel like work. Live life according to what you think your purpose is. The best way to focus on your purpose is to find out what you're naturally good at doing—something you can do more easily than most individuals.

Bill Gates, Steve Jobs, Warren Buffet, Mark Zuckerberg, Oprah, Will Smith; what do these people have in common?

They had natural gifts, built on it, found a way to make a living out of it, and found how other individuals could benefit from it. While this isn't the ultimate formula for happiness, it gives you something to look forward to every day.

Mental Health Savage challenge

Take a picture of yourself doing something that you love and are passionate about. For example, a picture of you cooking, a picture of an art project you are working on, poetry, gardening, helping others, etc. the options are limitless. Use hashtag #Ballingwithmypurpose

Find a political environment that matches your beliefs

When I began writing this chapter, I thought about all the multiple ways politics has influenced our culture. Politics affects the housing sector, the banking sector, the academic sector, the religious sector, the food sector, the medical sector, etc. Every single sector that politics affects indirectly affects our mental health, whether we like it or not.

If you grow up in an environment where politicians are not making favorable decisions to your wellbeing, it is only natural that you will face stress. Let use the current political climate in the United States of America as an example. Most individuals fall under two categories: Republican or Democrats. If you are a democrat in a republican climate, you're most likely not going to be too pleased with the public policies going on around you.

If you believe that abortion and a woman's right to choose what happens to her body is okay, you might not be too pleased to live in a State with strict anti-abortion laws.

If you believe in fair distribution of wealth, you might not be too pleased living in a state where the rich barely get taxed as much as the middle or lower class.

It is difficult to change the stripes on a zebra. We all have individual beliefs, and that's fine. However, if someone else's belief negatively affects your life, I firmly believe you should do something about it. If you need to protest, protest. If you need to move to another city, state, or even country that is more inclined to your beliefs, do so.

Every continent, country, state, county, city, and even street is different. There is a reason why we don't all have the same hobbies. There is a reason why we don't all have the same tastes in food. We all have preferences, and it is okay.

A prime example I would give is a gentleman I came across a few years ago. He is an African American man living in one of the most conservative states in the U.S. He has faced multiple racially provoked situations. He has been followed around the store. He has been called the N-word. He sometimes fears for his life and avoids certain roads due to fear of the police. He has been turned down on jobs because of his race. He feels like he never gets his voice heard politically because votes are all about the overwhelming majority.

He is constantly in a state of anxiety, and he doesn't even know it. He has gotten so used to the discrimination and the fear, it is part of his lifestyle. Unfortunately, conscious and unconscious anxiety is guaranteed to affect your physical health, eventually.

Another example is a lady I met from Utah. She is from a strictly traditional home and strictly traditional State. As fantastic as the idea of women's rights is, it isn't a pleasant topic in the family she is from. One day, she gathered the courage, after discomfort, to move to a different state. She began a whole new life.

Last example, access to educational opportunities differs

from State to State and from country to country. In some places, scholarships are readily available, and in other places, scholarships are not. Access to scholarships and grants is mainly political. It is all based on the priorities of the political climate you live in. Access to good education is also based on the environment you live in. A client of mine had to make a vital decision to move out of the state he lives in, leave his family behind because the educational prospects he was seeking didn't meet his financial means.

Sometimes, for our mental health, we will need to move to a better political climate. Watching the news alone is stressful. You hear about policies being changed, taxes being increased, dysfunctional government etc…and all you want to do is cringe and hide in the bathroom because you know you have no choice but to adapt. Some cities favor the middle class, and other cities don't. Some counties favor the upper class, and others don't. Find your political place—a place where your beliefs don't make you a stranger or target. Find your peace.

Another major thing that needs to be focused on is voting. Voting allows your voice to be heard. Voting allows you to choose who is the best candidate to help increase your quality of life. Unfortunately, people are more focused on presidential elections than other "minor" elections. The mayor of your city is important, and so are those who sit on the city council. They make pertinent decisions that affect your quality of life.

The senatorial and house of Representatives elections are as important and possibly more important than the presidential elections. They make significant laws that affect your income and taxes.

Do not let the 1% control how your quality of life is. News media have almost successfully convinced the population that their votes don't count. It does.

My point is every political position matters more than you know. Invest time researching who the politicians around you are, their policies, and what they stand for. You would be surprised to find how much of their work affects you.

Remember, politicians, work for you, not the other way around.

Mental Health Savage Challenge

Research political policies that have increased your stress levels and quality of life. Write a letter to your senator about ideas to make a change and always vote. To create more accountability, tag the politicians on your post on social media. #PoliticsandMentalHealth

Find a religious environment that matches your spirituality

#MySpiritualityMyPower

Religion plays a significant role in our lives. It determines what makes us feel guilty, sad, regretful, and angry. It also determines what makes us happy and joyful. Your religious beliefs play a significant role in your sense of morality, what you eat, what you wear, how you speak, your perspective, and even how you sleep. Religion is a big deal.

However, there is a difference between religion and spirituality. In my opinion, religion is nothing but organized spirituality. Spirituality is simply your connection to your higher power, while religion is the set of rituals you do to connect to your higher power. You may be religious and not spiritual. You may be spiritual and not religious. In this chapter, I'll be focused on both because both are a part of the *organized whole.*

In 2009, I questioned religion for the first time. Before then, my life revolved around the church; school, volunteer work, friends, and family. I didn't question Christianity in itself. I examined all the things that had to happen for Christianity to exist. Then, I began to venture into other religions like Islam and Buddhism, etc. Then I stopped and realized that every religion on earth had a central theme; believe, be good, pray, and hope for good things to happen to you. However, various religions have become more apt to do what the foundation is against—to judge others.

Soon after, I leaned away from religion and became more spiritual. It put me in touch with my higher power, and it also gave me a sense of peace because I was less focused on all the rules of my religion and more focused on having a relationship with my higher power. The act of religion is like going to school to learn what you can learn by yourself.

This is where mental health comes in. If you are Christian and haven't broken any of the ten commandments, come see me whenever possible. If you are Muslim and haven't broken any of Allah's requirements, see and talk to me. If you are any of the religions and haven't veered away from the path it has created, you are unique. But that's not the reality. We are all flawed creatures. Therefore, when things happen that go against our religious beliefs, we might feel anxious, threatened, angry, and even depressed. Being judged by others tends to affect a person's self-esteem and, eventually, overall mental health.

I have met a woman who loves piercings but won't do it because it goes against her religious beliefs.

I have met a gentleman who has had two kids out of wedlock and is desperately anxious because he has broken his religious rules.

I have met a child who lied and is overwhelmed by tremendous guilt.

I have met an elder who is depressed because of past sins that overwhelm her. Yet her religious beliefs worsen the symptoms.

In life, we can only do our best and try to be as perfect as our religion demands, but we can't always be perfect. What

Tami Odimayo

matters is our connection to our higher power.

I am not telling you to stop going to church. I'm telling you to focus on spirituality more than religion.

Having a higher power balances our spirituality. It doesn't always have to be focused on religion. It could be focused on anything. If you get your spirituality from water, for instance, sitting by a lake might be more beneficial than being in a temple.

Find your spirituality, find your power.

Mental Health Savage Challenge

Everyone's spiritual place is unique. Take a picture of your spiritual place or something that demonstrates your spirituality. #MySpiritualityMyPower

ACKNOWLEDGMENT

Psychology is my passion, but I would never have discovered it without Professor Telan and some of my undergraduate professors. I am grateful for the recommendation to switch my major from pre-med to psychology. It is a leap of faith that I am eternally thankful for.

To my beloved parents, thank you for your emotional and financial support throughout my learning career. All those pep talks didn't go unheard for sure. Thank you for having faith in me.

To my friends, if I had a dollar for every time I tried to be a therapist instead of a friend, I'd be a millionaire. Thank you for tolerating me.

To my girlfriend, thank you for encouraging me to write this book instead of binge-watching my favorite shows.

To my readers, I appreciate your support and responses to this book so far.

Helpful Resources

National Institute of Mental Health (NIMH) provides information on statistics, clinical trials and research. NAMI references NIMH statistics for our website and publications (866-615-6464)

The American Foundation for Suicide Prevention provides referrals to support groups and mental health professionals, resources on loss, and suicide prevention information (888-333-2377)

The National Domestic Violence Hotline provides 24/7 crisis intervention, safety planning and information on domestic violence (800-799-7233)

The Suicide Prevention Lifeline connects callers to trained crisis counselors (800-273-8255)

Anxiety and Depression Association of America (ADAA) provides information on prevention, treatment and symptoms of anxiety, depression and related conditions (240-485-1001)

Children and Adults with Attention-Deficit/ Hyperactivity Disorder (CHADD) provides information and referrals on ADHD, including local support groups (800-233-4050)

Depression and Bipolar Support Alliance (DBSA) provides information on bipolar disorder and depression, offers in-person and online support groups and forums (800-826-3632)

International OCD Foundation provides information on OCD and treatment referrals (617-973-5801)

National Center of Excellence for Eating Disorders (NCEED) provides up-to-date, reliable and evidence-based information about eating disorders (800-931-2237)

Schizophrenia and Related Disorders Alliance of America (SARDAA) offers Schizophrenia Anonymous self-help groups and toll-free teleconferences (240-423-9432)

Sidran Institute helps people understand, manage and treat trauma and dissociation; maintains a helpline for information and referrals (410-825-8888)

Treatment and Research Advancements for Borderline Personality Disorder (TARA) offers a referral center for information, support, education and treatment options for BPD (888-482-7227)

Printed in Great Britain
by Amazon